CLINICAL INTERPRETATION OF THE
Wechsler Intelligence Scale
for Children (WISC)

CLINICAL INTERPRETATION OF THE
Wechsler Intelligence Scale
for Children (WISC)

ALAN J. GLASSER, Ph.D.

California State College, Long Beach, Long Beach, California

AND

IRLA LEE ZIMMERMAN, Ph.D.

Whittier Psychological Center, Whittier, California

GRUNE & STRATTON   New York and London

GRUNE & STRATTON, INC.
111 Fifth Avenue, New York, New York 10003

Library of Congress Catalog Card Number   67-11952
International Standard Book Number   0-8089-0151-6

Printed in the United States of America

CONTENTS

INTRODUCTION

What is intellectual functioning? How does it reveal itself? While on the surface these questions appear to be separate and discrete, in reality they are no more than two ways of asking the same thing, for we can have no idea of a person's intellectual potentiality except by measuring what he does. Undeniably, hereditary and constitutional factors do operate to produce nervous systems which are capable of differing responses, and hence varying degrees of what we call intelligent behavior. However, the only way in which we can come to know and measure these differences is in terms of certain tasks and operations. While it may be undeniable that basic qualities of intellectual capacity "exist" within the brain, as the study of "primary" mental factors has attempted to demonstrate, all that is known is how these hypothetical factors show up in life situations, among which are those involving the use of intelligence tests. Thus, for practical purposes capacity is no more than a construct.

IMPORTANCE OF NON-INTELLECTUAL ASPECTS

Rather early in test development it became apparent that non-intellectual factors may contribute as much to test results as those "purely" intellectual, and to this end numberless personality tests have been devised. However, in the excitement that attended the ascendancy of the individual personality test, the "non-intellectual" aspects of intellectual functioning were, for the moment, forgotten. These aspects of performance were neglected in assessing the results of intellectual tests like the WISC. Examiners in general, and school psychologists in particular, were urged to obtain a "number" by which they could classify an individual and so dispose of him. A current study of institutionalized individuals later found to be of normal intelligence stands as a sad reminder of this era (Garfield and Affleck, 1960). The original protocols contained pertinent references to non-intellectual factors (for example, "child tested immediately after death of mother") which were then ignored. By the 1940's, this tendency began to give way to an increasing recognition that non-intellectual factors not only influence test scores, but may actually be discovered in the test behavior and raw data of the protocols produced by subjects. Today the essential intermingling of affective and intellectual factors in a complex matrix is accepted by all serious students. One of the purposes of this book is to delineate, separate, and assess the importance of these factors.

1

TESTING IN SCHOOLS AND CLINICS

By the year 1920, psychologists were first engaged by the schools for the very clearly limited job of psychometric examination of children to be placed in special classes. The growth of more general intellectual testing in the schools can be typically traced to this introduction of special training classes. Many states made placement in these classes dependent upon the child's rating on standard psychological tests administered by qualified examiners. These individuals came to be known as school psychologists, and were increasingly employed to meet this requirement.

As conceptualization of interpretation of test results has developed in current thinking, the notion of *level* of intelligence has become progressively less important. An individual IQ test for the purpose of getting a number is not only excessively time consuming for the psychologist, but actually of minimal value. That a youngster is of average ability may be comforting to the parent—but why can't he read? That another boy is of high average ability can be duly recorded in his school "cum" folder—but how can his disruptive behavior in the classroom be managed? What we tend to be more and more concerned with, then, is the application of what we learn of the child's cognitive and affective processes as they relate specifically to various kinds of home and classroom behavior.

When studying school-age children, the primary concerns have become the evaluation of intellectual performance and potential as they interact with the world and the learning process, and the ascertaining of how personality factors affect this potential. Since time is an ever-present aspect in determining what can be done in the test situation often a sound and well-administered intelligence test is virtually the only test which can be used regularly. This being the case, it is our aim to demonstrate that many of the important personality variables which affect classroom performance and general functioning can be gleaned from this one test. If such a procedure is possible, an economic yet valid personality assessment can be achieved.

Psychological testing should be used as part of practical decision-making, not merely to confirm what the parent or classroom teacher already knows about the child. Two children who present the same behavior at home or in the classroom may be motivated very differently and thus require different handling. One child, for example, referred for "day dreaming," may turn out to be a seriously disturbed, pre-psychotic youngster, drifting farther and farther from reality. Another, with the same symptom, could be extremely concerned with reality: the approaching separation of his mother and father. In both cases, responses given to the WISC can be used to make a meaningful distinction, and to indicate the necessity for completely different management of these children.

REFERRAL PROBLEMS

What are some of the basic problems for which children are referred for psychological testing? Summarized, they are:

SCREENING FOR MENTAL RETARDATION: The educable mentally retarded child (IQ 50-79) often must be screened for placement in special classes. Here testing may confirm the obvious. However, for administrative reasons, a "number" is usually needed for these children. The arbitrary quality of "cutoff points" (below IQ 80—special class; IQ 80 or above—regular class) is obnoxious to all, parents, teachers, administrators, psychologists. Too often, no distinction is made between the child's *need* for special training and his "numerical" qualification for such a class. Also, no *number* can differentiate between present functioning and potential intelligence, as in the case of a child whose emotional problems affect his memory, problem-solving ability, and other functions.

One of the advantages of the WISC for screening the mentally retarded child is that not only can the level of intelligence (IQ) be obtained, but that a careful interpretation of the total test will allow for the much more significant description of the child, his functioning and his potential. From this information, educational planning and possible psychotherapy can be determined.

THE SLOW LEARNER: The slow learner of average or above average intelligence is an ever-present problem to the psychological examiner. Whether the blocks are in reading, mathematics, spelling, or other specific areas, or whether a diffuse problem exists where not much of anything in the classroom seems to be absorbed, the WISC can point the way to specific emotional or perceptual problems, which are contributory to, if not root causes of, the scholastic deficiency.

BEHAVIOR DISORDERS: Another large group of children who are of constant concern is labeled under the general rubric of behavior problems. Problem behavior ranges from manifestations of rebelliousness and frank expression of hostility on the one hand, to withdrawal or isolation on the other. Since the motivation for such behavior almost always resides outside the classroom situation, it is necessary for the examiner to probe below the surface actions of the child as seen in the classroom or with his peers. For example, the teacher may represent symbolically a hated or resented significant figure from the child's family constellation. When tests make this clear, and separation between symbol and reality can take place, the problem has a chance of being corrected.

BORDERLINE PROBLEMS: There is one elusive group of children who represents what may be termed borderline problems. That is, these children are apparently not living up to potential either in terms of scholastic or behavioral standards, yet reasons for this are far from clear, with few or no clues available. Psychological testing can sometimes indicate the problems which are involved in the management of these children.

Psychological testing at its best can help penetrate beneath the surface manifestations and point the way to sensible decisions based on intimate knowledge of the child and his motivations. Only in this way can psychological testing be made to serve its highest and most important function in the school setting.

The day of the global, hazy, impressionistic approach—"Test this child and let me know what you find out!"—is passing. Psychologists are not concerned with "blind diagnosis" as a sort of psychological parlor game. Instead, they attempt to foster a close working relationship between psychologist and parent, doctor, or teacher. The testing service must outlive the day when it is a place to which a child can be "sent" (often with the implication of a trip to Siberia), and from which an impersonal report is delivered to the referring doctor, teacher, or the like.

TEST SELECTION: OVERVIEW OF THE WISC

Of all the tests available to the psychologist, the Binet and the WISC are far and away the most widely used. The Stanford Binet L-M has had a long priority in the field in its various forms, and, since it covers a wide range of two to eighteen years, is of great value in the schools. The age range assures a lower 'floor" and higher "ceiling" than the WISC, leaving the Binet the test of choice for two groups of children: the severely retarded (particularly IQ's below 50), and the gifted. Also, the Binet is recommended for the younger child. However, the newly introduced Wechsler Preschool and Primary Intelligence Scale (1966) will extend the age range of the WISC (since it is a downward extention of this test) from four through seven. This is particularly helpful to the examiner, since the WISC tended to subject the young child (below age eight) to continuous failure situations due to insufficient items easy enough for him.

The WISC is certainly as useful as, if not superior to the Binet for children of normal intelligence from ages eight to fifteen. Some of its advantages are listed below.

An outstanding characteristic of the WISC is the verbal-performance breakdown of subtests. This facilitates testing of the physically handicapped, such as the blind, deaf, or the orthopedically handicapped. At least a portion of the WISC will usually prove administrable to such a child, and with the subtest format, this portion, at least, can be used as an estimate of ability. By the same token, the culturally handicapped, such as the bilingual child, can be given non-penalizing parts of the test. Further, a comparison of verbal and performance results can be utilized as a rough measure of the degree of handicap, such as limited English knowledge or motor impairment, which is present.

The subtest format of the WISC helps to prevent or, in any event, to ameliorate the sense of frustration resulting from the administration of item after item beyond the comprehension level of the child, such as is required in order to establish the "ceiling" of the Binet. Also, administration time is standardized, permitting a more efficient use of the psychologist's schedule. If time is especially short, various forms of the WISC, such as the brief test using several subtests rather than all eleven, can be used in a much more flexible way than can the Binet.

The greater diversity and range of tasks in the various subtests make the WISC more valuable than the Binet, which places an undue emphasis on abstract verbalization at various age levels. This diversity also keeps motivation high and provides face validity both for the child and for those with whom the results are to be discussed.

The interaction effects of fatigue and failure upon the child as he reaches the more difficult test items are to some extent vitiated by the

WISC, with its progression of equally weighted subjects. This is in contrast to the Binet, which has all the most difficult items occurring at the end of testing rather than at different periods within the examination.

Pattern analysis of subtests as a way of distinguishing diagnostic categories, such as the "neurologically handicapped" or "poor reader," has proved unsuccessful with the WISC. What can be extremely meaningful, however, is something first discussed by Rappaport et al. (1945) and Schafer (1948), and endorsed here, namely, that the *kinds* of successes and failures or mistakes, rather than statistical treatment of scores, offers us a qualitative, phenomenological profile of personality attributes of vital significance. This point, the "how" of test responses rather than the scores per se, cannot be overemphasized.

WISC norms and standardization are comparable if not superior to the Binet in terms of applicability to the average range of the United States population. WISC and Binet reliability also are comparable. The advantages of an IQ based on a standard score rather than on the mental age is evident by its adoption for the new Stanford Binet L-M. Particularly for the older child, the elimination of awkward corrections for the differences between chronological and mental age is a blessing.

LIMITATIONS OF THE WISC

The standardization sample of the WISC, while excellent for the area covered, is too narrow in scope, concerning itself only with white, mainly middle-class children. Other groups, such as the Negro, the Mexican American, and such culturally deprived as migratory workers' children were excluded. Yet these groups are often those most in need of help and most frequently referred for examination. Further, the number of cases used at the ends of the ranges of intelligence and of age as well was too small. For this reason the test is best applied to children in the middle ranges of both age (8 to 13) and intelligence; the extremes are not as adequately measured as on the Binet. For instance, it is possible for a five year old child to achieve an IQ of 52 on the WISC while scoring zero on all subtests. It is not until age 12 that a raw score of zero does not receive some credit as a weighted score on at least one subtest. Also, a survey of WISC versus Binet scores of gifted children suggests that when children are rated on the Binet as having IQ's in the 160's, their

WISC scores will average over 20 points lower (Lucito and Gallagher, 1960).

In many ways, the WISC is essentially a revamped Binet, composed of various tasks (most of which are also found on the Binet) which are assumed to be components of intelligence. The WISC is thus based solely on the pragmatic inferences about the nature of intelligence first advanced by Binet. The rationale for interpreting subtest scores remains obscure. The provision of equal weighting of all subtests at all ages overlooks the fact that different aspects of intellectual functioning are measured by the same items at different ages (Cohen, 1959).

One of the greatest problems with the WISC (and now equally true of the Stanford Binet L-M) is the absence of an alternate form, essential in retesting. As a stop-gap measure, the Wechsler Bellevue Form II has been employed. However, this test is useful for ages 10 and over only, and suffers because the WISC is actually only an extension of this test.

Finally, the complicated wording and emotionally laden items on some of the subtests affect the validity of the WISC. A number of the items on the Comprehension subtest involving such issues as cutting one's finger and getting into fights are affectively charged, while "government positions" and "organized charity" are examples of overly complicated wording. This emphasizes the need for examining the meaning of item failures ("testing the limits") when administering the WISC, particularly in cases where cut-off points are needed, so that particular scores may not prove unfairly penalizing.

SUMMARY

The present book will have as its focus practical applications of knowledge about the WISC which it is hoped will maximize the use of this test for the examiner. Major areas of interest to be covered will include detailed instructions on administration and scoring procedures, material on the projective aspects of the WISC, an analysis of each subtest in which each of these will be analyzed both extensively and intensively, a summary of Brief Test Forms of the WISC and, finally, comments on reporting results and interpreting protocols.

REFERENCES

Cohen, J.: The factorial structure of the WISC at ages 7½, 10½, and 13½. *J. consult. Psychol.* 1959, 23, 285-299.

Garfield, S. L. and Affleck, D. C.: A study of individuals committed to a state home for the retarded who were later released as not mentally defective. *Amer. J. ment. Defic.* 1960, 64, 907-915.

Lucito, L. and Gallagher, J.: Intellectual patterns of highly gifted children on the WISC. *Peabody J. Educ.* 1960, 38, 131-136.

Rappaport, D., et al.: *Diagnostic Psychological Testing*, Vols. I & II. Chicago: Year Book Publishers, Inc., 1946.

Schafer, R.: *The Clinical Application of Psychological Tests.* New York: International Universities Press, 1948.

I

ADMINISTRATION AND SCORING

ADMINISTRATION

The complexity of the behavior to be found in any seemingly obvious test situation could occupy many pages of description. What the examiner must seek as he administers the test is an overall clinical impression of the child, and the child's reaction to the interpersonal situation involved in testing.

There are three important aspects of this clinical impression which overlap and are not at all mutually exclusive: The examiner's attitudes and behavior in the test situation, the child's attitudes and behavior, and the degree of rapport which exists between examiner and child.

EXAMINER VARIABLES: A knowledge of human psychology points to the conclusion that complete objectivity on the part of the examiner is a meaningless abstraction which in any concrete case does not exist. To say this is not to deny the need for such objectivity as is possible, but merely recognizes that examiners are human beings rather than automatons, and that they have their own needs which can, unless understood to some degree, powerfully affect the child's productions and the test interpretation. In the performance of his duties, the examiner satisfies basic needs such as security (he is the one asking the questions), self-gratification (he knows the answers) and the esteem of others (he is the expert to whom they look). Yet the child for one reason or another may thwart the examiner's needs by giving vague, evasive or otherwise unsatisfactory answers. The resulting anxiety and resentment on the part of the tester may lead to his making overbearing demands on the child, demands which can wreck the testing situation. For instance, the tester may be "helpfully" condescending, or overly friendly, or cold and aloof, or irritable and impatient. In any case, rapport is destroyed. In a sense one prys into another's life by asking him to answer questions and perform tasks, and inadequate realization of this can increase the anxiety of both child and examiner. There is a fine line between making the child comfortable and being overindulgent; between acting firm enough to get the necessary information and flexible enough not to alienate the subject. The very fact that they are in charge tends to arouse guilt in some examiners and leads to a diffidence which limits

9

their efficiency both in administration and utilization of test results. This can also lead to resistance and resentment on the part of some subjects who are keenly aware of their "inferior" status as children.

Some examiners are socially inhibited. A too personal approach by the child can cause them to withdraw defensively, and again effectively destroy a sense of community. Others have strong needs for approval which they cover up by smothering the child with solicitude and failing to insist upon his best efforts. Still others may be coldly intellectual, so that the testee feels like a specimen in a glass jar— "an interesting case." Finally, there are those whose hostility, though repressed in themselves, appears in the form of encouraging "naughty" behavior on the part of the child. If, as an examiner, one is at least partially aware of traces of such tendencies in oneself (and since they are universal, we all have some of them), it becomes immeasurably easier to guard against their affecting test performance and results.

CHILD VARIABLES: The child's response to the examiner and the test is the obverse of the situations described above. How does he face the loss of control inherent in the situation? Is he able to stand up to the confrontations of the examiner and to those self-confrontations which may become painfully obvious as the test proceeds? Do his dependent or approval-seeking needs get out of hand? Is he dependent on or resentful of help, and can he make constructive use of such help? A good rule of thumb is to note any initial flow of talk, since normally a child is at first somewhat reserved in the testing situation.

ESTABLISHING RAPPORT: Rapport is a highly complex state of affairs and, moreover, one which can change rapidly in the course of the testing in response to any of the many variables just discussed. How can rapport be achieved and maintained? Obviously a purely mechanical set of instructions or "gimmicks" can never do the job. Two conditions are necessary and both spring from the personality of the examiner: A genuine warmth toward and interest in the child, and at least a partial knowledge of one's own personality assets and liabilities. Given these, problems of rapport largely resolve themselves.

One suggestion that may be helpful is to begin the examination by asking the child what he knows of testing (why he is being seen), clarifying his misunderstandings and briefly explaining the purpose of testing: "Do you know why you are being seen by the psychologist? . . . No, it doesn't mean you are crazy (or stupid or bad). We want to find out some things about you, what you know, and how you think. We have seen a lot of children. This test will help us . . .," etc. Free conversation, following the lead of the child, can then be used to introduce testing.

Some examiners use the Draw-A-Person Test as an ice-breaker; this can prove helpful. However, for the school-age child, the WISC subtests themselves are an ideal beginning.

Sample instruction for the WISC are as follows:

"I will be giving you this test which, as you see, is divided into eleven parts (here demonstrate this by showing the selections on the blank). Each part starts out with easy questions which then get harder as we go along. This is because the test is made up to test children from the first grade on, up through high school. Don't worry if you can't get all the questions right—I don't expect you to. But I do want you to do the very best you can."

As for sequence of administration of subtests, giving them in the order of appearance on the record blank is more than satisfactory, as well as complying with WISC standardization. Information and Comprehension items are a simple and non-threatening introduction to the test materials tending to produce a "classroom" set. When the child initially asks if a certain task was done correctly, or demands to know the answer, it is best to avoid giving a direct response. "Fine!" rather than "Correct" frees the examiner from responding to answer after answer. If this cannot be done without spoiling the rapport, an answer can occasionally be given the child. Intermittent, casual encouragement is helpful in obtaining maximum results. Directions and administration must be standardized as noted in the WISC manual. Still, there will be times when the examiner must depart from the given instructions in order to achieve meaningful results. All eleven subtests should initially be given, although for compelling reasons of convenience a short form may sometimes be utilized.

As the test proceeds, certain techniques to encourage the continuance of good rapport and the best possible performance have proved to be of value. A good knowledge of all possible scorable responses to an item is indispensable; then, if in doubt, one can ask for more information. Children may be encouraged to handle the stopwatch if they wish, and it should be left in sight—this reduces their anxiety about it and their awareness of it. On timed items, it is often best not to take the task away until the child shows some discouragement and frustration; otherwise allow him to work a bit overtime on the item until he does it correctly.

With some children the examiner may find it helpful not to stop after the final failed item in any particular subtest, but to complete the series. In this way surprising potential may sometimes be ascertained, although points accrued cannot enter into the final scoring. Active help on any item can, of course, be given only after failures on any particular subtest have reached their limit. The question of help is a difficult one, chiefly because to date there is no alternate form to use for retest. Sometimes, however, the need to know *now* about the child's level of functioning or potential over-balances the retest probolem. It must be emphasized that standardized administration, though important, need not be slavishly followed in a difficult case. Here the examiner must use all his imagination and resourcefulness in order to derive worthwhile results from the testing.

Note Taking

One suggestion to be recommended is that the examiner write his notes while the child is engaged in testing, and just after he leaves. Letting the material become stale can result in the loss of many important clues. Always write down verbatim all the material given to Information, Comprehension, Similarities, Vocabulary, as well as the stories given to Picture Arrangement and unusual answers to Picture Completion.

Asking the child his birthday and age allows the examiner a standard opening and a chance to check on the child's knowledge of this "overlearned" data. Disturbed, acting-out children often reveal their immaturity and problems by giving much extraneous material here ("I don't know my birthday. Nobody told me. They won't give me a party." etc.).

Initial notes can be made both when asking for the birthdate and during the administration of Information. It is helpful to note the initial impression given by the child, including notations as to attractiveness, size, grooming, and the initial degree of apprehension.

The point at which extra questions are required on Information to bypass the child's quick "I don't know" can be noted with a simple "Q." These often give the clear evidence of the extent to which the child feels dependent, or to what degree he insists upon accuracy so that he will not even hazard a guess.

With Comprehension, as well as with Vocabulary, deviant responses may give important leads to the child's preoccupations. For example, does he find it difficult to accept the concept of (Item #1) a "cut finger" without being flooded with fears of amputation and hospitalization?

On Arithmetic, the child's thought processes can be better understood by inserting a simple "how is that?" to an unusual answer.

Responses to Similarities often give an estimate of "set" and readiness to abandon an unsuccessful approach to a task. For example, children may insist the two items are NOT the same but they are opposites. Or a bright child may strain to reach a high level of abstraction (a "two" answer) on the later items so that over-inclusive responses are given (for example, paper and coal are chemical compounds) while ability to switch to a more concrete level at this point would improve the child's score.

Throughout the entire test, guessing should be encouraged on the easier items. As a general rule "Don't know" must not be accepted until it is clear that the child has reached his upper limit. Children can be urged to try, particularly when obviously simple items are rejected. Responses to such urging can reveal important personality variables. Perfectionists as well as those whose confidence is easily shaken are unable to take advantage of the encouragement. Personal irrelevancies tended to creep into replies of some children as pressure increases.

At the upper limit, it is well to offer the child an occasional face-saving device, such as, "You haven't had that yet?" The child's ability to use these devices and to react to failure should be noted. Some children realistically accept not knowing, others must be given assurances. A disturbed child may insist that he should know all the answers. A dependent child may recall this "aid" on the next subtest, and insist with the most simple item that he "hasn't learned that yet." Performance at the upper limit permits assessment of self confidence (for example, freedom to guess) as well as reality testing retained by the child when reaching his maximum.

Extension Testing

Giving such help to a child as may be necessary to get a more accurate picture of his potential has been termed *extension testing* (see Taylor, 1959; Volle, 1957), since this includes extending efforts beyond the instructions given by Wechsler. Roughly speaking, three levels of help can be distinguished. First, an initial refusal to answer is not accepted—at least a try, even though a guess, is insisted upon. Second, more specific help is indicated when questions are repeated, and encouragement is given, such as pointing out the child's ability along a certain line ("You just got the last one"). Third, a graded series of suggestions or hints can be employed systematically to explore the degree of structuring necessary to elicit a satisfactory response. These will vary with the subtest. The value of extension testing is to help the examiner understand a *specific* faiure or weakness in an otherwise adequate test. If a child has difficulty with most of the WISC, it is obvious that another test should be substituted (for example, Stanford Binet) and the WISC can then be saved for administration when the child has reached a more appropriate mental age. There can be no substitute questions which receive credit in the scoring. Extension questions are best based upon the child's own apprehensions or difficulties. For example, if the child says at Comprehension (Item #1, "cut finger"), "Go to the hospital," the item can be rephrased "just a little cut."

Suggestions about the specific subtests follow.

INFORMATION: Initial questions can be phrased in the third rather than the first person in order to make them impersonal or generalized. For example, #5, "What must you do to make water boil?" can be rephrased, "What does your mother do . . .?" "What are the four seasons" can be made easier by asking, "What season is this?" or "When do we have vacation? . . . Fine, now give me the rest of the seasons."

COMPREHENSION: Perhaps nowhere else in the WISC is rephrasing more valuable than on Comprehension. Not only are the items loaded with potentially traumatic material, but some call for a specific vocabulary (for example, #10, "government positions—examinations"; or #11, "organized charity") which tend to rule out the items for bright young children who are quite capable of understanding the concept, if not the specific vocabulary. Here, as noted above, questions should be geared to the child's difficulty. On the train-item (#5, "broken track"), the child might respond to the following: "The train will be wrecked if it hits the broken track. What can you do?" #10, "government positions—examinations," can be reworded as "Why should we give tests to people who want jobs with the government?" Great flexibility is demanded, since testees and test circumstances can vary greatly.

ARITHMETIC: To obtain a more adequate evaluation of numerical skills, Arithmetic items can be extended readily. With the initial block counting, the child might be asked for two blocks (mental age 3 years) or four blocks (mental age 5 years). Also, restating the initial problems as "Give me 4 . . . give me 7," rather than the "Take away all but . . ." format, can be helpful. The next question, #4, can be reworded readily, first to clarify, then to simplify the questions: "What does it mean, to cut something in half? . . . Then how many would there be?" For #5, "How much is two pennies and two pennies? Four pennies and two pennies?" At #6, one can ask the child how much 8 plus 8 is. If the answer is correct, return to the original question. On the next item, the same method can be used: "If a boy sells 5 of 10 papers, how many are left?" Then return to the original. On #8, the multiplication problem, the child can be asked if he knows any "times" tables. If so, the answer may then come easily to him. The same method can be used on the division problem. The "oranges" problem, #12, can be simplified by asking how much is 30×2 and 30×1, then repeating the entire question. #13 can be hinted at by asking how much is $\frac{1}{2}$ of 36. In 14, stressing the importance of the 3 pencils as a unit may help the child see the number of units contained in the 24 pencils. The taxi problem solution lies in the computation of how much 4 quarters of one mile will cost, at 5c a quarter-mile. Finally, the key to the last problem may lie in stressing the words "after each deal" and reminding the testee it is not merely a matter of dividing 27 by 3.

SIMILARITIES: Again, extension questions must be based on the child's misperceptions. The "set" of the child is most often involved in failures (#5, "Plums aren't yellow, and peaches *are*").

If the child says the items are not alike, it is often possible to return to #3, "knife and glass," which is much easier, and by using the child's similarity ("cut" or "break"), show the child that he has said how those two were the same, "Now, how are cat and mouse the same?" Further help can be given by introducing other analogies. In view of the book familiarity most children have with farm animals, for instance, one might ask how a cow and a pig are alike. Or, for pound and yard, substitute quart and inch; drum and gong for piano and violin; and so on.

VOCABULARY: On Vocabulary items, the words can be set in a meaningful sequence: "A spade in a garden—what is *that*?" Also, the varied meanings of a word can be hinted at. An advantage of extension testing on Vocabulary lies in thus getting around the unwillingness of some children to define a word except by a synonym.

DIGIT SPAN: Here, the child who is unable to say three digits forward ("Say 1, 5, 7") can be given two digits forward, or numbers in sequence ("Say 1, 2, 3"). Digits backward can also be given in sequence ("Say 2, 1 backwards"). Also, the child's response to extra trials is worth exploring.

PICTURE COMPLETION: Initially one should follow Wechsler with the admonition, "Yes, but what important part is missing?" the first time an erroneous part is given. Demanding close and sustained attention will itself result in many more positive answers ("Look at the whole picture").

PICTURE ARRANGEMENT: Here, particularly in a case marked by early failure, it is essential to get the child to verbalize the stories. In this way it can be seen if a correct idea was marred by faulty execution, or if the child simply did not comprehend the story. Questions directed to the child about specific aspects of the story may then elicit latent comprehension. Another way to test this is to arrange the pictures for the child, then immediately scramble them and ask for reproduction.

BLOCK DESIGN: In Blocks, several very simple patterns (for example, 4 reds) can be introduced to evaluate initial failures. Later, demonstrating the design for the child is probably the best way to see if he can successfully complete the task. The whole design should be reproduced for the 4-block patterns. The designs may be taken away or, at a more simple level, left for the child to follow. For the more intricate patterns, doing only a part of the design allows the examiner to see if the child can follow a lead. Another method which is recommended is the substitution of Kohs Designs (obtainable from Psychological Corporation, N. Y.) This consists of a series of pictures which become more and more obvious with respect to the composition of any particular design.

OBJECT ASSEMBLY: Again, partial or complete reproduction by the examiner can be used in testing the limits. Also, verbal hints can be employed ("Where are his legs?").

CODING: Directing the child on each symbol (point from each number to the chart) can simplify Coding. Also, use of a second copy of the code may help some children, especially if they are allowed to place it where they please. For older children, a try on the simple Coding A may give some picture of the child's difficulty.

For a better understanding of difficult cases, selected tests from the Binet can be added to the battery, for instance, memory for sentences, absurdities or other items involving judgment, similarities and differences, verbal recall, etc.

SCORING

Perhaps the most obvious and yet crucial point about scoring is the necessity to use the manual constantly in determining a score for any particular item. Too often, examiners rely on their memories to establish scores and, as a result, report IQ's which are completely invalid. The most experienced examiners still use the manual for scoring every WISC administered. Massey's Supplement (1964) is most helpful for questionable items.

Scoring should rarely be done while the test is in progress, since this distracts the examiner from recording necessary observations. However, a good knowledge of the criteria for all items is demanded of the examiner, since he needs to know when to request more information ("Tell me more about it") and when this is not necessary. It is well to keep in mind the WISC instructions for eliciting further responses. Too much demanding violates standardization and can artificially alter the scores, particularly on Comprehension.

A particular scoring problem is raised by the presence of multiple answers. The following is a rule of thumb: If the child gives a correct answer plus something irrelevant or neutral, the answer can still be scored plus. If, however, a correct answer is given, and then an incorrect one is substituted, the response is spoiled and must be scored minus. Asking the child which of the two answers is meant can be helpful in understanding the child but still must be scored minus. If both correct (Level two) and incorrect answers are given as alternatives to a question, it is scored one.

Particularly in scoring the verbal WISC, the examiner will face many instances when an answer seems clearly relevant and appropriate, yet no precedent exists for it in the scoring manual. Rather than score such a response zero and distort the score of the subtest, it seems reasonable to allow a score of one or even two for such answers. As Wechsler notes in the manual, simply because the child did not come up with the limited answers shown in the manual is no reason to penalize him. This suggestion requires judgment on the part of the examiner. Most particularly, he needs to avoid a mere "halo" effect. Deviant answers may sound more "reasonable" when produced by verbal little blonde first-graders. On the other hand, to fail to give credit to unusual responses can result in an unnecessarily low IQ. It must be kept in mind that the WISC scoring is not "objective" in the sense of requiring only specific responses to the verbal tests. Sterility, not objectivity, results when there is too slavish adherence to instructions and rigid, limited scoring. Testing is administered to allow an understanding of the child, not to derive a mechanical IQ. When significant increases in IQ are observed on retest, it is of value for the examiner to study the original protocol. Repeatedly, inadequate, mechanical scoring and ready assumptions of the child's inability to cope with the test material merely because he refuses to answer questions spontaneously will be observed to have resulted in a spuriously low IQ.

ADMINISTRATION AND SCORING SUGGESTIONS

Administering and scoring are two of the most important phases in utilizing any test. Carelessness or errors at this stage invalidate the most perceptive interpretation of results. The following suggestions may prove helpful.

ARITHMETIC: On items (2 and 3 counting) asking the child to place blocks he "takes away" on a piece of paper nearby can simplify recognition of which blocks he meant to leave for himself.

Since Arithmetic is a measure of number concepts, if the subject indicates the numerical amount but with the wrong label, his answer should be considered correct. For example, on item #6, if the child answers "7 magazines" (instead of "newspapers") this is credited plus.

DIGIT SPAN: A major problem in administering digits is to prevent the younger child from repeating the numbers as they are said, and not waiting for the examiner to finish the series. Sometimes it is possible to grasp and press the child's hand while numbers are said, thus focusing his attention, letting go to indicate the series is completed. Saying as instruction, "I am going to say a group of numbers," will often avoid this difficulty for older children. For younger children the expression, "I am going to say some numbers together," or simply stopping the child and saying, "'Wait until I finish," will handle the problem.

PICTURE COMPLETION: The issue here is for the child to indicate what is missing. Pointing should be encouraged. Inaccurate naming of the missing item is not penalized.

BLOCK DESIGN: Copying the design involves correct position of the design as well as accurate block placement. Initial rotation on A, B, and C can often be corrected by asking the child upon completion, "Is it exactly like this?" (model or picture). If this fails, the examiner can rotate the blocks correctly to conform with the design, then ask the child to reconstruct the design again (score one if then correct). Initial attempts to make the sides as well as the top match the model can be blocked by saying, "No, just the top—not the sides." For some children, it is worthwhile to place the model in the box, thereby concealing two sides. This helps a child who perfectionistically insists on "total accuracy."

OBJECT ASSEMBLY: Scoring problems arise when juxtapositions must be scored, but the object is not totally assembled. In the case of the Auto, a theoretical score of 6 could be achieved in this manner. However, it should be noted that a maximum of only 5 points may be attained for an incomplete design.

CODING: An admonition to the child not to erase or worry about neatness can be included in the instructions. If the subject then erases during the performance proper, he can be reminded to go ahead instead.

REFERENCES

Massey, J. O.: *WISC Scoring Criteria.* Palo Alto, Calif.: Consulting Psychologists Press, 1964.
Taylor, Edith M.: *Psychological Appraisal of Children with Cerebral Defects.* Cambridge, Mass.: Harvard University Press, 1959.
Volle, F. O.: A proposal for testing the limits with mentally defective for purposes of subtest analysis of the WISC verbal scale. *J. clin. Psychol.* 1957, 13, 64-67.

II

REPORTING W I S C RESULTS

Without sound, positive communication of test findings, there is little meaning in the procedure of testing. Yet it is often at this point that the whole enterprise falters and becomes lost in a thicket of confusion. Assuming a reasonable ability of any examiner to express himself in current, colloquial English, there still remain certain pitfalls to be avoided, and certain aspects of reporting to be emphasized.

One of the commonest problems in report writing is the examiner's predilection for a certain favored hypothesis. L'Abate (1964) applies Bruner's (1951) theory of hypothesis strength to testing. Although designed for other purposes, this hypothesis seems to fit the present discussion rather precisely. The stronger the hypothesis (in the examiner's mind, in our case), the greater is the likelihood of its arousal from the test protocol. The stronger it is, the less objective evidence will be needed to confirm it. Finally, as a corollary, the amount of inappropriate behavior needed to refute it will increase in direct proportion to the strength of the hypothesis.

Hypothesis strength in the mind of the examiner is determined by a number of things, among them the paucity of alternative ideas, the frequency of confirmation in the past, and the fact that certain hypotheses suggest specific action to be taken by or for a particular child. All too often, however, these stem from fashionable trends in interpretation, such as the current enthusiasm for the waste basket category "brain-damaged," or from a poverty of theoretical background in the examiner. Whatever the source, if the examiner is aware of the possible error stemming from inappropriate attachment to a hypothesis, a long step will have been taken toward more objectively meaningful reports.

The first essential feature of any report is a clear presentation of the reason for the examination, specific questions to be answered (for example, "Should this child be considered for special class placement?"), and a brief description of presenting problems which led to the referral (for example, "cannot master school assignments" or "does not pay attention in class").

The referral material is a fundamental guide for establishing what questions can be answered by the test data. Unless these questions are formulated as a guide to help determine what to look for, the report can very easily become rambling, vague, and general, or even irrelevant. By contrast, when the referring teacher, administrator, or clinician requests quite specific information, the task of interpretation is much easier and more meaningful. "Blind" interpretations make interesting tours de force, but cannot make a maximal contribution to understanding the child. Actually, the same symptomatic behavior noted in many referrals can have many different sources.

What these statements suggest is the need for much closer liaison and rapprochement between the examiner and the referring source. These latter people (teacher, pediatrician, principal, for example) need to be briefed on the sorts of questions which can and cannot be answered by testing. For instance, the statement, "Give a personality appraisal," is so broad as to become meaningless, while, "Give some psychometrics—an IQ test—the TAT," is so narrow as to be infuriating to a conscientious examiner. On the other hand, some hypotheses the examiner formulates may also be so general as to be quite useless, for instance, "This child is disturbed," or "This child is brain-damaged."

The importance that test material may have for subsequent analysis is also a factor, since the test report may in the future be consulted to answer very different referral problems. The clarity of the original presentation will determine the use made of the examination at a later date. A standard example is a child originally referred for consideration for special education. His brief attention span and difficulty in controlling himself in the classroom are specifically mentioned as referral problems. On examination he is found to be of average intelligence, and the case is closed. Several years later, a second referral may be made, on the basis of apparent emotional problems in the classroom. The initial test, sought to answer one question (mental retardation), now may give important information as to earlier emotional or behavioral problems, and changes in the child's adjustment over the years.

In planning the test report, the following preliminary steps are essential: First, identifying data should include name, age, sex, birthdate, grade level, date(s) of examination, examiner's name and *position,* and the source of referral.

Second, the introductory material should usually contain a brief review of the child's background, including reference to all other referrals for evaluation. Relevant material for this section would include physical status, emotional well-being, family background, including number and age of siblings, psychological problems outside of the school setting (or their absence!), prior school adjustment, and previous test data. The latter is particularly important. Readministration of a WISC one month after original testing is certainly of little value. Knowledge of previous testing would allow the examiner to decide whether further testing was actually required, or to select a valuable alternate test for the second administration. The whole history should be summarized in one or two brief paragraphs, so that it can be reviewed quickly as it bears on test results. A reference referring the reader to a separate case study can be inserted if necessary.

In considering qualitative features of the report, several areas require emphasis. A careful description of the child's attitudes toward testing, as well as his verbal and non-verbal behavior (including interaction with the examiner) during the test session, is essential. This should include objective observations of the child, as well as impressions which could be inferred as a result of these observations. These may be compared to the reasons for referral which were previously noted. For example, a child referred as distractible or hostile in the classroom, may prove to be tractable and disarming in the test situation. Inferences might then be made as to such factors as the child's response to individual attention, a male examiner rather than a female teacher, the implications of authority, or even of a specific hostility between teacher and child which would be resolved in a class transfer.

Among the kinds of behavior which should be observed in the test situation are variables described in detail in Chapter IV on projective aspects of the WISC, including such points as attention, concentration, attitudes toward the examiner, attitudes toward the test material, amount of confidence, and degree of personal reference. From such material, clues can be elicited which lead to considerable insight in understanding the referral problem. From these observations the adequacy of testing can be inferred. A specific reference to the desirability of retesting immediately or at a later date will bring out clearly the examiner's judgment that present testing is not considered definitive.

Following the above sections should be the main body of the report: Test results, interpretation, and conclusions. Here, there is a strong temptation to succumb to the wizardry of numbers—the WISC IQ, the weighted subtest score, the percentiles, the number of standard deviations from average. The majority of persons to whom the test report is addressed have only a hazy, often incorrect understanding of the meaning of these numbers. Yet because numbers are concrete and "objective," these will often be emphasized as the key to understanding testing. In the process, qualitative communication which accompanies these magic numbers and which will be of real importance in understanding the child may be completely ignored. Therefore, numerical interpretations should be used sparingly, properly qualified and explained.

Recognizing this, what specific numbers should be used in the test report? Those which seem reasonable are the IQ's (full, verbal, and performance), since this provides the reader with a standard shorthand estimate of overall intellectual functioning, and, depending on the reader, a profile summary of test performance, based on age equivalents or weighted subtest scores. Such a profile can be drawn on the table presented by Wechsler (1951) covering ages 5½ to 15½. By age equivalent is meant the following: Any child, regardless of age, achieving a specific weighted score, such as 8 on Information, is scoring at a level expected of the average 7½ year old. (A summary of age equivalents for all WISC subtests can be found in the sample charts, pages 34-35. Estimates of what are considered significant differences from average are given in Chapter III, Subtest Analysis.)

In a school setting, the overall intellectual functioning should be given at the start of the test evaluation, preferably in a paragraph standing alone, and qualified in terms of the adequacy of measurement. Thus, the WISC could be reported as follows:

John is functioning at the average level, with verbal skills only slightly better than performance skills (WISC full scale IQ 103, verbal IQ 105, perf. IQ 99). However, the wide variability in his responses, including his failure to respond to simple items when he could successfully answer more difficut questions, indicates that present functioning is limited, and under other circumstances he should function at the bright normal level or better.

Objective evaluation of the child's present functioning level is necessary, together with inferences about potential or ultimate level of functioning. At this point, considerable caution should be employed before inferring any major lack of or loss in ability. Current studies of schizophrenic adults whose test results from grade 2 are available indicate that the present level of functioning, while low, is consistent with early testing (Lane and Albee, 1965). Often, the examiner attempts to differentiate between functioning and potential intelligence as a kind of magic talisman which protects him from mistakes in evaluation. A classic example is labeling a severely autistic child as "potentially superior," with the unstated qualification that he must first receive and profit from ten years of intensive residential care. When potential intelligence is estimated, the examiner must indicate what conditions must be fulfilled for the child to reach this potential. These conditions might vary from "further time to establish rapport with a shy and immature child" to "reduction of anxiety so that this boy is able to attend to the test."

Turning from present and potential estimates of intellectual level, L'Abate (1964) has suggested a helpful rubric for analyzing and understanding the subject's performance.

1. How does the subject present himself? (appearance, test attitudes, etc.)
2. What is he really like? (cognitive and affective functioning, defensive maneuvers, etc.)
3. Why does the individual behave the way he does? (underlying determinants)
4. How and when, historically, was the behavior acquired? (environmental background)

If these questions can be thought of as general guidelines rather than as specific report subheadings, and if care is taken to cover them all at some point in the report, a thorough, meaningful analysis will be forthcoming.

In most cases, careful analysis of the record will reveal a major theme running through the material, clarifying the pattern of high and low scores, or the general level of functioning. For instance, "this boy's difficulties seem to stem from an impoverished background, as indicated by his difficulties with . . ." or "crippling anxiety appears to be the major reason for the poor performance of this girl, as revealed by her nervous gestures and responses on . . ." A clear statement of the theme can thus be documented by relating relevant aspects or testing to it. A catalog of specific strengths and weaknesses will be seen to arise from such an analysis, since it gives the writer a loom upon which can be woven the threads which constitute a rounded evaluation. Relevant emotional problems must be stated, as well as the child's characteristic defensive structure or attitudes, since these play major roles in cognitive functioning.

There must be great caution in reporting results by naive translations of test scores into statements about the child (for example, a
low Information score reported as "a limited fund of general information"). Reference to factorial studies of the WISC (see Cohen,
1959; Lotsof, 1958) reveal the dangers of drawing pat conclusions
from small subtest differences. By the same token, it is essential to
avoid technical discussions of subtest differences in the report. Such
discussions confuse the reader and add nothing to the report.

Another point to be stressed is the avoidance of meaningless phrases
translated directly from the subtests, with no attempt to relate the
material to the referral problem. "Rote memory" is mentioned by
Huber (1960) as a particularly meaningless phrase. By contrast,
since factorial studies indicate that Digit Span is a good measure
of attention at certain ages (see Cohen, 1959), such an interpretation can be used when appropriate.

Above all, as Huber (1960) has stressed, statements must be explicit. Jargon should be avoided, while overqualification of findings
make them meaningless, causing the reader to question their inclusion in the report. One way to avoid this problem is to put more
factual and less inferential statements in one section of the report,
and put the more speculative items in a separate paragraph, properly
labeled as tentative. However, clinical reports are not essentially factual, but carefully thought out inferences from *one* sample of behavior. Often when the writer finds himself qualifying excessively,
he might consider whether a written report is desirable in this case.
Some of the most overly qualified reports are those written to un-
informed readers. A simple report of a test of intelligence is hardly
the place to educate a lay reader in such intricacies as the implications of the standard error of estimate, or the variability possible in
the Comprehension score of a dependent seven year old.

Particularly important is the relating of actual test findings to the
so-called non-intellectual factors observed during the test session and
recorded in the protocol itself; this can be helpful in presenting a
valid picture of a particular child. An example of this is the test of
a child who has serious problems in attending. When his attention
is captured momentarily, he shows signs of average intelligence. Yet
the inability of the examiner to elicit good responses except by cajol-
ing and anchoring the child to the task must be pointed out in the
report, and the inference that such a child can not begin to reveal
his potential in a crowded classroom must be spelled out. If this is

not done, the psychological report will be filed away as proving that Johnny could learn if he "wanted to" because he has a good IQ, and the teacher, with encouragement from the inadequate report, may mark Johnny off as a "lazy boy, who just won't try."

Following the body of the interpretation, there can be a brief summary of the test results and interpretation, in a sentence or two, a device which serves to sharpen the impression given by the report as a whole. As a general rule, diagnostic labels should be avoided, since categorization at its best, by nature of often gross overlapping of groups, can be most misleading. Further, a child may carry an inaccurate or oversimplified label with him like an albatross throughout his school career, while the rationale (or lack of one) for such labeling has been forgotten. Such labels as "autistic" and "brain-damaged," given with scant evidence, can be particularly disabling. These labels, placed on a child by an unsophisticated examiner, have often automatically excluded a child from psychotherapy or remedial programs.

The next paragraph in the interpretation is concerned with those conclusions drawn from the testing performance which are related to the presenting problems and case history. Thus, "The child's erratic test functioning and overall poor performance is due to a lack of confidence in his own ability. This in turn seems to have been engendered by a history of constant depreciation by the father, according to the case study." Throughout the test interpretation, such inferences must be drawn, and if necessary, reasonable speculation indulged in.

The last section of the report covers the recommendations of the examiner. Here is the crux of the examination: Namely, assuming that the child is functioning in a particular way for a listed number of reasons, what can be done to help him? Recommendations can be addressed to teachers, parents and others. In this connection, regular time should be set aside for teacher-psychologist conferences after the teacher has read the original report. Such conferences allow the teacher to explore methods of following through on recommendations, and allow the school psychologist to venture his more tentative hypotheses or speculations as to the child's behavior which go beyond those based on the original examination. Getting to know the teachers and others who refer children can lead to the improvement of reports. Communication as well as mutual respect will be vastly improved in this way.

Recommendations for teachers include such items as what can be expected of the child in the regular or remedial class, and what the teacher can do to handle emotional problems with understanding. Specific recommendations of change of teacher, class, or school, or of exclusion may be made. Mentioning special disabilities and abilities can aid the teacher in setting up an optimal learning situation for the child. Thus, test findings indicating that this is a child who relies on a concrete, down to earth approach to the world may lead to specific recommendations on the presentation of school material.

Recommendations for parents may deal with such matters as study practices, types of discipline, and standards for achievement on the one hand, and suggestions for parent and child counseling or psychological referral on the other. The recommendations must be realistic and practical, rather than idealized suggestions which can never be achieved. One way to assure this is to give a sliding scale of recommendations: For example, "This child shows so much anxiety that intensive psychotherapy is clearly indicated. Since this is unlikely to be available locally, the parents might be referred to a family agency for counseling. Even if this suggestion cannot be followed, a minimum number of demands in the classroom would perhaps serve to keep the level of anxiety as low as possible. Also an active, sympathetic interest on the part of the teacher may heighten this child's self esteem and lead to greater success in school work, with resulting self confidence. . . ."

To summarize the major points in writing test reports, the following should be stated:

1. Insist on specific referral questions.
2. Be aware of your own hypothesis biases.
3. Include relevant identifying material and background data.
4. Always include in the main body of the report test results, interpretation and conclusions.
5. Use only numbers pertinent for the purpose, no more.
6. Remember to always ask four cardinal questions:
   How does the subject present himself?
   What is he really like?
   Why does he behave the way he does?
   How and when did he acquire this behavior?
7. Organize the report around a major theme.
8. Finish with summary and recommendations, taking care to make the recommendations realistic.

The sample report form and test writeup on the following pages illustrate the foregoing principles.

REFERENCES

Brunner, J. S.: Personality dynamics and the process of perceiving. In Blake, R. R. & Ramsey, G. V., Eds., *Perception: An Approach to Personality*. New York: Ronald Press, 1951.

Cohen, J. The factorial structure of the WISC at ages 7½, 10½, and 13½. *J. Consult. Psychol.* 1959, 23, 285-299.

Huber, J. C.: *Report Writing in Psychology and Psychiatry*. New York: Harpers, 1960.

L'Abate, L.: *Principles of Clinical Psychology*. New York: Grune & Stratton, 1964.

Lane, Ellen A. and Albee, G. W.: Childhood intellectual differences between schizophrenic adults and their siblings. *Amer. J. Orthopsychiat.* 1965, 35, 747-753.

Lotsof, E. J., Comrey, A., Bogartz, W., and Arnsfield, P.: A factor analysis of the WISC and Rorschach. *J. project. Tech.* 1958, 22, 297-301.

Wechsler, D.: Equivalent test and mental ages for the WISC. *J. Consult. Psychol.* 1951, 15, 381-384.

PSYCHOLOGICAL EVALUATION

NAME   DATE OF REPORT
AGE   SCHOOL
SEX   GRADE PLACEMENT
BIRTHDATE   DATE(S) OF EXAMINATION
                                        EXAMINER'S NAME & POSITION

REASONS FOR EXAMINATION & SOURCE OF REFERRAL
(Specific questions to be answered by examination)

RELEVANT HISTORY AND FAMILY BACKGROUND

TESTS GIVEN
(Note previous testing)

DESCRIPTION OF BEHAVIOR IN TESTING SITUATION
Objective reporting of child's verbal and motor behavior
Inferences

TEST RESULTS AND INTERPRETATION
Evaluation of intellectual functioning
a. Profile summary of test performance (chart)*
Full scale IQ, Verbal scale IQ, Performance scale IQ
Mental age performances in all subtests
Overall intellectual functioning (short summary paragraph)
b. Positive or strong factors, potential vs. actual functioning
c. Negative or weak factors
Evaluation of social-emotional aspects of the personality and re-
lationship to intellectual functioning

SUMMARY: CONCLUSIONS AND RECOMMENDATIONS
Brief summary of overall findings
Recommendations for:
a. Classroom adjustment
b. Assistance with personality problems
c. Parental and sibling relationships

---

* See examples, pp. 34-35.

SAMPLE TEST WRITEUP

PSYCHOLOGICAL EVALUATION

Name: Lee P.
Age: 10 years, 11 months
Sex: Male
Birthdate: Dec. 25, 195–

Date of report: 12-3-19–
School: Jefferson Elementary
Grade: B-5
Date (s) of Examination: 11-25-19–
Examiner: George Moore, M.A.
      School Psychologist
      L.A. City Schools

Reason(s) for Examination

Lee, a transfer this year from another school district, has been achieving so poorly in his present classroom situation that his teacher has questioned his capacity for successful fifth grade work. Testing is requested to determine whether Lee needs special academic placement or if his potential is at least average and other factors are responsible for his current academic lag. No behavior problems are mentioned.

Relevant History and Family Background

Lee is the younger of two sons (brother, George, is 17) of parents in their early 40's. Both parents are college graduates; the father is head of his own successful engineering consulting business. The relationship of the parents is apparently good; there are no reports of any serious clashes between them and either child. The parents have indicated that the older boy has also been an academic problem recently. Father reports some trouble with his temper when the boys do something of which he disapproved. The standards of both parents, particularly Father, are high.

Lee's school history began at age 5 in a parochial school where the classes were extremely large. After two years of virtual non-achievement he was sent to a military school, where, according to the mother, he continued to achieve little or nothing. He detested the military school. Capitalizing on this, Mother has threatened to return him to military school if he doesn't "straighten himself out" in his present situation.

Health history is non-eventful and general health is excellent. As for Lee's emotional adjustment, the parents report him to have been a quiet, cheerful child with no problems beyond his school difficulties. However, in the past year he has begun to lie and to avoid responsibility. He also started a small fire in a trash can near the house.

There is no previous test data.

Description of Behavior in Testing Situation

This handsome boy, with clear skin, regular features and gray eyes, greeted the examiner tangentially, glancing nervously around the room before he sat down at the desk. From the beginning he was overconcerned with his performance, requiring much urging and repeating many times in the course of the examination, "It's the best I can do," "It's hard," "I can't do it." Of one Arithmetic problem he noted, "If that was in a book, I'd go on to the next page." He also wondered whether he was given trick questions. Several times he got up and examined objects in the room; he also gazed around frequently. If unsuccessful in a task his behavior became erratic, even panicky. For instance, he piled the pieces to be assembled one on top of another. Upon conclusion of the testing, Lee heaved a sigh of relief and all but tore out of the room.

Test Results and Interpretation

Lee's full scale I.Q. of 95 would place him in the average range of intelligence (Verbal I.Q was 97, Performance I.Q. 93).* However, these summary scores have little or no meaning in understanding Lee, because they mask his wildly erratic performance. Thus he is functioning at the six year level in rote recall of numbers, and at the 16 year level in being able to form verbal abstract conceptualizations, while the remaining scores are scattered in between.

From Lee's remarks, behavior, and disorganized handling of verbal and non-verbal materials, he seems to be suffering from the effects of crippling anxiety. From his responses it is clear that this anxiety centers around feelings of hostility, aggression, and independence which Lee is unable to express directly. Instead he adopts a passive attitude to handle these feelings. For example, when asked what should be done if a boy much smaller than himself started a fight with him, he replied moralistically, "It wouldn't be proper to fight—I don't like to fight." If sent to the store to buy a loaf of bread when the grocer didn't have any, he passively concluded that he'd just go home. Again, when shown a simple 3 picture prize-fighting sequence of cards he was unable to arrange them correctly, although he did much more difficult sequences without trouble.

Summarizing, from the wide scatter between subtest scores (6–16 year levels), as well as the scatter within individual subtests, it appears that Lee when functioning near his best is of bright average intelligence. (His I.Q. would then be 110-115). The reason for his anxiety lies in his inability to resolve his hostile wishes in an acceptable manner. The small fire that he started recently is an example of an unacceptable solution.

Conclusions and Recommendations

Lee is doing poorly in school for a number of reasons. Lack of intelligence is not one of them, since he has the capacity to do at least average work. Rather, his present performance is a consequence of various historical and

---

* This result, if interpreted at face value, would be an excellent example of the danger of concrete dependence on test numbers, particularly those which are composite scores, such as the WISC I.Q.

personality factors: inadequate preparation in fundamentals, unhappy school experiences, a history of non-achievement, very high parental standards, parental threats, and crippling, repressed hostility. As a result of the combination of these factors Lee's attention and concentration are seriously impaired and his present poor achievement is the consequence.

Intensive help in fundamentals, together with psychological counseling for Lee and his parents, is recommended.

/s/ George Moore, M.A.
School Psychologist

WORKSHEET FOR TEST WRITEUP

Here we will attempt to show the roots from which the interpretation was derived in the case of L.P.

A. Notes on Behavior.

Overconcern on part of subject—necessity for urging.
Feelings of inadequacy and wanting to give up.
Feelings of wanting to avoid problems altogether.
Suspicion of examiner.
Anxiety in the test situation, expressed in panicky, erratic movements, much looking around, problems of concentration.

B. Notes on Test Results.

Present overall functioning level—average. Extremely uneven quality indicates danger of taking this as his potential—danger of dependence upon concrete numbers. Weighted scores range from 6 (Digits) to 15 (Similarities). With this spread, and the small number of subtests (11) it is futile to try to calculate an average subtest weighted score. His extremes range from the 6-year level (rote recall of numbers) to the 16-year level (verbal abstract conceptualizations).

(Note: It is always useful to compare in terms of age level, rather than weighted scores alone).

Evidence for overt anxiety: Test behavior as noted above, particularly disorganized handling of test materials. The anxiety stems from certain feelings he is unable to express directly: (1) Hostility and aggression. Evidence: Answer to comprehension "fight" item, "It wouldn't be proper to fight—I don't like to fight." In Picture Arrangement, he was unable to arrange the prize fight sequence correctly, although he did more difficult, non-aggressive sequences correctly. (2) Overdependence. On the "bread" item in Comprehension, he concluded he'd just go home. His overriding tendency in both areas is to adopt a passive solution or express resentment in an extremely roundabout way (note starting of fire—historical material brought in here).

His potential is definitely higher—probably between 110 and 115.
Evidence: Inter-test and intra-test scatter, stemming from anxiety-disrupted performance.

C. Notes on Conclusions and Recommendations.

Poor school performance is not due to lack of intelligence—at least average work can be expected.

Present functioning due to various historical factors—poor preparation in fundamentals, high parental standards, parental threats, history of non-achievement, repressed hostility.

Intensive remedial help plus psychological counseling seems indicated.

Name _____ Date _____ Birthdate _____ Age _11-9-16_

School _____ Grade _6_ Teacher _____ Examiner _____

C.A. _11-9_   Verbal Scale I.Q. _99_   Performance Scale I.Q. _108_   Full Scale I.Q. _104_

TESTS	AGE EQUIVALENTS											TEST MEANINGS
VERB. TESTS	5½	6½	7½	8½	9½	10½	11½	12½	13½	14½	15½	
1. Inform.	5	7	8	10	11	13	14	17	18	19	20	Information from experience and educ.
2. Compre.	5	6	8	9	11	12	13	15	16	16	17	Practical knowledge and social judgement
3. Arith.	3	4	5	7	8	9	10	11	12	12	12	Concentration and arithmetic reasoning
4. Simil.	3	4	6	7	8	9	10	11-12	13	13	14	Logical and abstract thinking ability
5. Vocab.	15	18	21-22	25-26	28-29	32-33	36-37	39	43-44	45-46	47-49	Word knowledge from experience and educ.
6. D. Span	5	7	8	8	9	9	10	10	10	11	11	Attention and rote memory

PERF. TESTS	5½	6½	7½	8½	9½	10½	11½	12½	13½	14½	15½	
1. P. Compl.	6	7	8	9	10	11	12	12	13	13	14	Visual alertness and visual memory
2. P. Arrang.	4	7-9	14-16	22-23	25-26	27-28	29	30	31-33	34	35-36	Interpretation of social situations
3. B. Design	4	5	6	9-10	13-15	16-20	21-24	29-30	32-33	34-35	36-39	Analysis and formation of abstract design
4. O. Assem.	8-9	12-13	14-15	17-18	19-20	21-22	23	24	24	25	26	Putting together of concrete forms
5. Code A.	17-20	28-31	35-37	40-41	44-45	46	47	48	48	48	48	Speed of learning and writing symbols
Code B.	-10	13-16	21-22	25-26	30-32	36-37	41	45-46	48-49	54-55	56-57	
6. Mazes	5	8	11	14	15	16	17	17	17	17	18	Planning and following a visual pattern

(Ref. D. Wechsler, Journal of Consulting Psychology, Oct., 1951, p. 382.)

Summary: _____

SAMPLE PROFILE SUMMARY OF TEST PERFORMANCE (not of foregoing case) (see pages 23 and 29)

Name _____ School _____ C. A. _8-7_ Grade _3_

Date _____ Teacher _____ Birthdate _____

Examiner _____ Age _8+_

Verbal Scale I.Q. _89_ Performance Scale I.Q. _92_ Full Scale I.Q. _89_

TESTS	AGE EQUIVALENTS											TEST MEANINGS
VERB. TESTS	5½	6½	7½	8½	9½	10½	11½	12½	13½	14½	15½	
1. Inform.	5	7	8	10	11	13	14	17	18	19	20	Information from experience and educ.
2. Compre.	5	6	8	9	11	12	13	15	16	16	17	Practical knowledge and social judgement
3. Arith.	3	4	5	7	8	9	10	11	12	12	12	Concentration and arithmetic reasoning
4. Simil.	3	4	6	7	8	9	10	11-12	13	13	14	Logical and abstract thinking ability
5. Vocab.	15	18	21-22	25-26	28-29	32-33	36-37	39	43-44	45-46	47-49	Word knowledge from experience and educ.
6. D. Span	5	7	8	8	9	9	10	10	10	11	11	Attention and rote memory

PERF. TESTS	5½	6½	7½	8½	9½	10½	11½	12½	13½	14½	15½	
1. P. Compl.	6	7	8	9	10	11	12	12	13	13	14	Visual alertness and visual memory
2. P. Arrang.	4	7-9	14-16	22-23	25-26	27-28	29	30	31-33	34	35-36	Interpretation of social situations
3. B. Design	4	5	6	9-10	13-15	16-20	21-24	29-30	32-33	34-35	36-39	Analysis and formation of abstract design
4. O. Assem.	8-9	12-13	14-15	17-18	19-20	21-22	23	24	24	25	26	Putting together of concrete forms
5. Code A.	17-20	28-31	35-37	40-41	44-45	46	47	48	48	48	48	Speed of learning and writing symbols
Code B.	←10	13-16	21-22	25-26	30-32	36-37	41	45-46	48-49	54-55	56-57	
6. Mazes	5	8	11	14	15	16	17	17	17	17	18	Planning and following a visual pattern

(Ref. D. Wechsler, Journal of Consulting Psychology, Oct., 1951, p. 382.)

Summary: _____

SAMPLE PROFILE SUMMARY OF TEST PERFORMANCE (not of foregoing case) (see pages 23 and 29)

III

SUBTEST ANALYSIS OF THE W I S C

A unique advantage of the Wechsler scales has been the grouping of test materials into twelve subtests, each of which yields its own weighted score. This allows an examiner to gather useful information with less than a complete test (brief forms of the WISC), and is also a factor in the more rapid administration of the WISC when compared with the Binet (an average saving of 13 minutes was noted in one study [Anderson, 1959]). The presence of grouped items into specific subtests also allows for serial measurements in a number of areas, and has led to the interpretation of the subtests in terms of special strengths and weaknesses as well as personality variables. Often these interpretations are, at best, naive translations of the subtests into such concepts as "memory" or "judgment." Even less defensibly, they may be based directly on findings extrapolated from the Wechsler Bellevue records of disturbed adults (Rappaport et al., 1946). While the WISC provides an excellent standard sample of child behavior, the prediction of specific types of behavior from subtest scores is open to considerable criticism. From the time of its introduction, Wechsler (1949) and Seashore et al. (1950) warned that the fairly low reliabilities of some of the WISC subtests make such interpretations extremely questionable, at least until the upper age levels (13 years), when findings are more likely to overlap with the adult Wechsler scales (Cohen, 1959). Even here, caution is essential. In one study, the WISC profiles of 50 children were compared with their profiles on the Wechsler Bellevue. The relative position of subtests was determined for both tests, and the similarity of profiles did not prove to be large enough to warrant prediction (Delattre and Cole, 1952).

In the following sections the subtests will be evaluated individually in terms of significant parameters. These analyses will begin with a brief description and history, rationale, and some conjectures on the contribution of the various subtests. Following this will be an analysis of item composition and difficulty which will relate raw scores and age level, as well as a review of the adequacy of item placement and difficulty in the light of current studies.

So-called scatter, pattern, or sign analysis has been utilized widely, but with even less than indifferent success. This appears to be be-

cause of similarities between the aspects measured by different subtests plus the overlapping in populations studied. Since variations
between the subtests are so often used as diagnostic "signs" despite
the above warnings, Hopkins and Michael (1961) analyzed differences found in the standardization sample, concluding, reasonably
enough, that the difference observed as actually occurring in a large
majority of the children is of questionable significance. Their findings
will be reported so that the examiner will have at his fingertips a
ready estimate of the likelihood of an observed difference to be expected by chance alone.

Two points, however, must be kept in mind. The purpose of test
analysis is to understand the child's approach to test material. A
comparison of statistical differences is only one portion of this. Thus,
even very large differences *can* occur by chance (in, for example, 5
cases out of 100), while very small differences can give a most valuable clue as to real variations in ability. Only careful analysis by a
skilled examiner can evaluate these two possibilities, which exist
above and beyond statistical manipulations.

Considerable reliance will be placed on the factorial analysis of
the WISC standardization data compiled by Cohen (1959). In his
study Cohen analyzed each subtest in terms of its contribution to a
measure of general intelligence (a general factor, G). Apart from this,
subtests were analyzed in terms of their contribution to factors which
were independent of the general factor, but were shared with at least
one other subtest (primary specific factors). Also they were analyzed
in terms of factors which were unique to each subtest (subtest specific factors) and finally for a factor attributable to subtest unreliability or random errors of measurement (error factor). The great
importance of this latter factor should be mentioned at this point
since a substantial degree of the variations from one subtest to another
can be attributed to nothing more than chance or fleeting changes in
functioning of the child being tested. Ignoring this point has led to
the often ludicrous "findings" of "organic patterns," and other statistical artifacts.

A further analysis of each subtest will draw upon the Guilford
Structure-of-Intelligence Components (Guilford and Merrifield, 1960).
Guilford has suggested that the total intellect can be perceived in
terms of three dimensions. The first is labeled *Contents*, or those
stimuli to which the individual reacts when he "uses his intelligence."
The second covers *Operations*, or the kinds of behavior observed

when one behaves intellectively. The third involves *Products,* or the kinds of behavior that result after operations take place on the different kinds of content.

Each of these dimensions is subdivided into mutually exclusive definitions. Thus, *Contents* is made up of Figural, Symbolic, Semantic, and Behavioral categories. *Operations* consists of Cognition, Memory, Divergent Production, Convergent Production, and Evaluation. *Products* consists of Units, Classes, Relations, Systems, Transformations, and Implications.

This complicated theoretical model has been applied to the WISC by Bonsall and Meeker (1964). Each item of each subtest has been categorized under combinations of the various kinds of factors, producing a three word description of the item in terms of the specific operation, content, and product involved. Many items are described predominantly by one factor, but several are described by as many as three.

Following the discussion of each subtest in terms of the Structure of Intellect model, there will be an evaluation of specific advantages and limitations of the subtest. Certain clinical judgments of the authors, their associates, and students, in the light of their own experience with the WISC, will be noted.

Each subtest analysis will conclude with a review of the interpretations advanced, screening implications which might be derived, and possible significance of high and low scores. These might refer to specifically high and low scores or again merely to an emphasis which might not even be reflected in objective scores. The ability to perceive such clues distinguishes sound test interpretation from a mechanical "cookbook" approach.

INFORMATION

Description and History

This subtest* consists of 30 questions in ascending order of difficulty, the first three being administered only to children below the age of eight or to older suspected mental defectives.

The type of question included requires a response using basic facts generally available to children within our society. Items of this type

---

* Chart I, page 41—and other subtests shown with Charts II-XII in this chapter— are reproduced by permission. Copyright 1949, The Psychological Corporation, New York, N.Y. All rights reserved.

were first included in intelligence testing in the Army Alpha Scale (Yerkes, 1921) which was devised and administered during World War I. At this time their empirical utility as a measure of intelligence was demonstrated. Since World War I questions of general information generally available within a society have been utilized with a high degree of success as a part of psychiatric interviews and as items for measurement on psychological group tests.

Rationale

This subtest assumes several points. One is that the questions included in this section cover a broad range of materials allowing an adequate sampling of information. The second is that such information may be acquired by an individual who experiences the usual opportunities in this society. The third is that the range of an individual's information is an indication of his intellectual capacity. The fourth is that more intelligent children have broader interests, greater curiosity, and seek more mental stimulation. It follows therefore that they should have greater amounts of the sorts of information available within the society. This information is primarily disseminated in the public school system, which in itself implies a degree of uniformity of general information available at the various age levels. Thus, the availability of a public school system is probably one of the most important factors in obtaining the type of knowledge necessary for successful achievement on this subtest. Such a school background, presumably available to all, is also the prime reason for the inclusion of this subtest in this intelligence scale.

What the Test Measures

This subtest is basically oriented to determine how much general information the subject has abstracted from his surrounding environment. The child is not asked to find relationships between facts but simply if he has obtained and stored them as general knowledge. This subtest calls into operation remote memory, ability to comprehend, capacity for associative thinking as well as the interests and reading background of the subject. Intellectual ambition as influenced by cultural background also is revealed by performance on these items.

Item Composition and Difficulty

This subtest includes several items of a practical nature which almost all individuals pick up from their common everyday experience. Items such as #4, "From what animal do we get milk?" and #6, "In what kind of store do we buy sugar?" are examples of information items drawn from general common everyday experience which is available to almost all individuals. Particularly the second half of this subtest, however, consists of items of information usually learned in school. Examples of this type of item are #16, "Who wrote Romeo and Juliet?" and #22, "What is the capital of Greece?"

Although common everyday experience and/or school attendance highly influence achievement on this subtest, success on these items also depends upon the age of the child. By turning to the manual, the average raw score which is expected for the child of $7\frac{1}{2}$ is eight or nine; for a child of $10\frac{1}{2}$, a raw score of thirteen; while a child of $13\frac{1}{2}$ is expected to have an average raw score of eighteen. While a scattering of successes usually takes the range of scores considerably higher, the child at $7\frac{1}{2}$ should have gathered enough information from his environment to answer the questions through the item pertaining to naming the days of the week #8 and who discovered America #9. The child of $10\frac{1}{2}$ should succeed through the item concerned with the direction which the sun sets #13. By $13\frac{1}{2}$ the child should be able to pass the items including the meaning of C.O.D. #18. This shows the excellent and wide range of items making up this subtest (Chart I).

Another area of concern for all those using the Wechsler is the particular placement of the individual items on subtests. Sutherland (1960) analyzed the item placement for this subtest to determine the adequacy of placement for children referred for study and between the ages of 7 and 15 years stratified according to the normal distribution of intelligence. From his findings he recommended only minor placement changes from Wechsler's original format for these items. For example his sample of "normal" referred children showed that item #7 ("How many pennies make a nickel?") is easier than item #6 ("In what kind of a store do we buy sugar?"). Thus, according to these results these two items should be reversed in order to have correct placement according to level of difficulty. Further evidence that the items are well placed comes from Carlton and Stacey (1955) who, using a sample of retarded children with an average intelligence quotient of 67, a chronological age of 12 years and an estimated mental age of 8, also did not find a need for revision of item placement. They did find, however, a sharp drop in achievement from the item asking for the four seasons (item #11) through the remaining

1. INFORMATION	Score 1 or 0		Score 1 or 0		Score 1 or 0
1. Ears		11. Season—Year		21. Pounds—Ton	
2. Finger		12. Color—Rubies		22. Capital—Greece	
3. Legs		13. Sun—Set		23. Turpentine	
4. Animal—Milk		14. Stomach		24. New York—Chicago	
5. Water—Boil		15. Oil—Float		25. Labor Day	
6. Store—Sugar		16. Romeo—Juliet		26. South Pole	
7. Pennies		17. Fourth—July		27. Barometer	
8. Days—Week		18. C.O.D.		28. Hieroglyphic	
9. Discoverer—America		19. American—Man		29. Genghis Khan	
10. Things—Dozen		20. Chile		30. Lien	

CHART I. INFORMATION SUBTEST

Guilford Factors

1. Memory for ideas
2. Memory for ideas
3. Memory for ideas
4. Verbal comprehension
   Associational memory
   Semantic relation selection
5. Verbal comprehension
   Associational memory
   Semantic relation selection
6. Verbal comprehension
7. Memory for symbol patterns
8. Memory for symbol patterns
9. Memory for ideas
   Verbal comprehension
10. Memory for symbol patterns
11. Verbal comprehension
    Associational memory
12. Verbal comprehension
13. Memory for ideas
14. Memory for ideas
15. Verbal comprehension

16. Verbal comprehension
    Associational memory
17. Associational memory
18. Associational memory
19. Semantic relation selection
20. Verbal comprehension
21. Memory for symbol patterns
22. Verbal comprehension
    Associational memory
23. Verbal comprehension
    Associational memory
24. Verbal comprehension
25. Verbal comprehension
    Associational memory
26. Associational memory
27. Verbal comprehension
28. Verbal comprehension
29. Verbal comprehension
    Memory for symbol patterns
    Associational memory
30. Verbal comprehension

Item placement of average scores for three age levels

Age 7½ (average raw score 8-9) success through item 8 or 9
Age 10½ (average raw score 13) success through item 13
Age 13½ (average raw score 18) success through item 18

items on this subtest. These last eighteen items did not add to the test's discriminative ability for this sample since few of these mentally retarded children succeeded in passing them.

In view of this finding, it perhaps might be valuable to add more items of a medium level of difficulty to help discriminate the upper levels of retarded children and the lower levels of the borderline-sub-normal children.

Significant Differences between Information and other Subtests

In order to obtain a statistically significant difference at the five per cent level between the Information subtest and any other subtest, Hopkins and Michael (1961) report that wide differences in weighted scores must exist. For comparison with the Arithmetic, Similarities, Vocabulary or Block Design subtests, there must be at least a difference of four weighted score points to obtain a statistical significance at the five per cent level. All other subtests, however, require a difference of five weighted score points or more from the Information subtest to yield this same minimal statistical significance.

Factorial Age Variables

When the WISC standardization data is factor analyzed (Cohen, 1959), the meaning and contribution of each subtest can be evaluated in its setting within the total test. The Information score, from this approach, is discovered to be an important component of the WISC. It is second only to Vocabulary in measuring general intelligence (the G factor) as this is represented by the full scale IQ score on the WISC. This is most marked at the older age levels ($10\frac{1}{2}$ and $13\frac{1}{2}$). At the younger age level ($7\frac{1}{2}$) this subtest, like all the others, tends to be so unreliable that as much as a third of the variability (average variance) can be considered as due to chance fluctuations.

Aside from its considerable contribution to the total score, a slight but consistent and solitary loading for Information has been shown on a factor which has been interpreted as "that aspect of verbally retained knowledge impressed by formal education" (Verbal Comprehension I).

For a young child, age $7\frac{1}{2}$, Cohen notes that an interpretation of the presence or absence of "specific verbal knowledge" might be inferred from the subtest when the score is quite deviant, that is, three points or more from his own general average. However, at the older ages such as $10\frac{1}{2}$ and $13\frac{1}{2}$, this specific type of interpretation cannot be made. And for all age levels, the proportion of the subtest score which can be attributed to an "Information" factor (known in factor analysis as "primary-specific," or reflecting the contribution of this subtest only) is practically nonexistent.

The Structure-of-Intellect components of Guilford and Merrifield (1960) have been applied to the individual WISC items by Bonsall and Meeker (1964) (Chart I). In their analysis they categorized the Information items under five different factors. The first and most common factor making up the Information items is Verbal Comprehension: To know the meanings conventionally attached to words in a language. The second consists of Memory for Ideas: To reproduce previously memorized intact ideas. The third is Memory for Symbol Patterns: To reproduce or recall interrelations among signs or code elements. A fourth and frequent item classification is Associational Memory: To remember meaningful associations of ideas. The fifth and final factor hypothesized, less frequent than the others, is Semantic Relation Selection: To select the relation most similar in meaning to a given or implied relation.

Only the first of these factors agrees with Cohen's findings, which are based on an actual factor analysis rather than on theory. The agreement as to the importance of Verbal Comprehension is in contrast to the emphasis on a memory component by Bonsall and Meeker. Even the labeled Memory subtest (Digits) failed to produce such a factor in Cohen's analysis. Therefore, the Structure of Intellect analysis of the WISC Information items must be seen as a theoretical and as yet unverified way of looking at this subtest.

Advantages

The initial advantage of Information is its value as an "ice breaker" in introducing the child to the WISC. Another advantage of this subtest is that it has an unusually good range of item difficulty. This of course insures achievement of some successes by almost every child, while at the same time it allows some failures even for the highest scoring children. Another advantage is that although a child has his initial exposure to failure on this subtest, he seldom finds such failure disturbing. Since the items often resemble school-type material, failure then can readily be accepted with the examiner's explanation of the range of items to the child. This procedure comfortably orients the child to the WISC serial testing format of each subtest running from easy to hard items. Where the subject has a record of school failure, the similarity of the questions on this subtest to testing of school subject material may give rise to reactions seen in the classroom. Items on this subtest basically represent typical school-influenced education, although it does measure more broadly based knowledge before age 7.

Generally items are emotionally neutral and rarely elicit an emotional response or personal reference. Finally, a not inconsiderable value is the rapid administration of this subtest.

Limitations

Because this subtest is so highly representative of typical school-influenced education in this country, children with foreign backgrounds usually are penalized in passing these items. This is equally true for children coming from culturally deprived environments such as those whose parents are migrant workers and the like. By the same token, children coming from extremely enriched environments may receive spuriously high scores. This should be kept in mind particularly for the very young child who receives large increments in weighted scores for every success above the mean for his age.

Summary of Interpretations

The Information subtest is often able to reveal clues to personality adjustment. Indications of verbal poverty or verbal fluidity may be revealed. Any tendency to give personal references or bizarre responses is rare on this subtest, thus of considerable significance. Information could spotlight the child who is afraid to know too much, the child avoiding reality, or the obsessive-compulsive child whose responses show excessive detailing.

Children who receive high scores on this subtest generally reveal a good memory and reflect an enriched background of a high cultural level with wide reading. High scores usually reflect an alertness and interest in the surrounding environment and suggest that this is a child who is intellectually ambitious. In fact, over-ambition may be shown in children scoring high in these items through their extended over-elaboration which may shade into an obsessive-compulsive detailing. In this connection, special note should be made of the child's inability to stop with conventional responses or of responses which have been reworked. A high score may also reflect an exaggerated need by the child to store information. This often occurs with children who equate knowledge with security.

Because of the ease of the initial items, a very low score on Information may be the first indication of a child with intellectual limitations or possibly even mentally deficient. If the mental age appears to be exceedingly low, the WISC probably, however, should be abandoned in favor of other test instruments more suited to testing children with low ability, such as the Binet. Low scores also can reflect other factors. A low Information score may suggest an orientation toward non-achievement, as is found in an impoverished environment; or it may reflect the attitude often relating to non-achievement that knowledge is a dangerous thing. Other possibilities of low scores can result from perfectionistic tendencies, or obsessive rewording of ideas which essentially lower the quality of the answer (for example, rejecting Columbus as the discoverer of America, or speculating as to whether the fourth of July was really the date of the signing of the Declaration of Independence). Hostility toward scholastic achievement, anxiety as shown by early "fails" and more difficult "passes," and orientation toward action rather than reflection may also be indicated.

COMPREHENSION SUBTEST

Description and History

This subtest of the WISC is composed of 14 problem questions designed to measure comprehension of behavioral situations, largely social in nature. The type of question included requires a response drawing on experiences which can be obtained by most children within our society. Sinilar items were first included as part of the original Binet-Simon intelligence scales. With the utilization of this kind of item on all subsequent Binet scales, verbalized comprehension of behavioral social situations has been demonstrated as one essential aspect of intellectual functioning.

Rationale

The underlying assumptions of this subtest consist of several related conceptualizations. Primarily, the subtest is based on the concept that social and "moral" behaviors are acquired (and utilized) by children through everyday living experiences as well as through school and formal education. Like Information, Comprehension items cover a wide variety of situations so that the range of the individual's comprehension presumably suggests his level of intellectual operation. Underlying a child's comprehension of social and/or moral behavioral development, however, is another assumption: children with greater ability, broader interests, and more curiosity will have a wealth of knowledge to draw from in solving the practical social problems presented to them in Comprehension. However, they still must synthesize their knowledge obtained from practical everyday experience or formal education in order to be able to cope with and to solve problems of social behavior.

What the Test Measures

This part of the WISC scale consists of an attempt to determine the level of a child's ability to use practical judgment in everyday social actions, the extent to which social acculturation has taken place, and the extent to which a maturing conscience or moral sense has developed. As seen by Wechsler, it requires use of so-called common sense judgment in a variety of situations. Success on this test probably depends a great deal on possession of practical information as well as the ability to evaluate and utilize past experience in socially acceptable ways. Success on this test also appears to be influenced by the child's ability to verbalize. Primarily this test is interested in determining if the child can use, in a socially accepted way, facts which he has gleaned from his surrounding environment.

The utilization of practical information in socially acceptable ways is a function of the appropriateness of thinking and to a high degree reflects the emotional state of the child. Thus the child's mode of approach in solving the problems presented in this subtest often reflects his emotional balance and stability. This can be assessed by the child's ability to avoid verbalizations of impulsive, anti-social, or bizarre behavior. It should be pointed out that this does not mean that such behavior will not occur simply because it is not expressed in words. However, avoiding poor responses and giving acceptable responses does indicate an understanding, even though possibly shallow, of the meaning of the social role. Of course, stereotyped, overlearned answers can conceal inadequate social judgment or a poorly developed moral sense. Responses to specific items may be very helpful in evaluating such factors as rational thinking and the delay of impulse expression. The makeup of the items which often stress injury or danger can readily evoke traumatic themes in the child.

In Table 1 some specific themes elicited by Comprehension items are listed.

This test allows for some sex differences to be observed, favoring boys, and reflecting the different roles that boys and girls play in our culture. Since boys are often more active in our society, they may be required to cope with more aspects of social behavior than

2. COMPREHENSION	Score 2, 1 or 0
1. Cut—Finger	
2. Lose—Balls (Dolls)	
3. Loaf—Bread	
4. Fight	
5. Train—Track	
6. House—Brick	
7. Criminals	
8. Women—Children	
9. Bills—Check	
10. Charity—Beggar	
11. Government—Examinations	
12. Cotton—Fiber	
13. Senators	
14. Promise—Kept	

CHART II. COMPREHENSION SUBTEST

Guilford factors

Items 1-5   Judgment
Items 6-7   Verbal comprehension
             Judgment
Items 8-14   Sensitivity to problems

Item placement of average scores for three age levels

Age 7½ (average raw score 8) success through item 4 or above
Age 10½ (average raw score 12) success through item 6 or above
Age 13½ (average raw score 16) success through item 8 or above

girls and thus are able to give more adequate answers to this part of the WISC than girls (examples here are #5, the train item, and #3, bread item).

TABLE 1.   CLINICAL SIGNS ELICITED BY COMPREHENSION ITEMS

Item	Possible Emotional Response Type	Examples
#1 What is the thing to do when you cut your finger?	Preoccupation with mutilation, punishment for disobedience, dependency on parents, phobias about blood, or injury in general.	"cut off your hand!" "shouldn't play with knife, you're bad" "tell mama"
#2 What is the thing to do if you lost one of your friend's balls?	Empathy, guilt feelings, carelessness, victimization, evasion of the problem, feelings of responsibility and following through.	"I'd give them all of mine" "tell them you didn't do it" "not do anything, not *my* ball"
#3 What would you do if you were sent to buy a loaf of bread and the grocer said he did not have any more?	Disobedience, dependence vs. independence, handling money fears.	"spend the money!" "ask your mother what to do" "tell your mother to get some" "I would be afraid to go to another store, might be kidnapped"
#4 What is the thing to do if a fellow much smaller than yourself starts to fight with you?	Acting out tendencies, excessive need to defend against tendencies to act out, denial of hostility, parental strictness, feelings about siblings.	"beat him up!" "let him beat me up" "like my brother keeps picking on me"
#5 What should you do if you see a train approaching a broken track?	Threatening responses, responses showing child's responsibility for act, guilt feelings, anxiety reactions.	"run away, might get hurt" "say I didn't do it, not *my* fault" "be scared" "watch it wreck up!"
#6 Why is it better to build a house of brick than of wood?	Destruction themes.	"all fall down" "people get killed"
#7 Why are criminals locked up?	Guilt themes, punishment themes, acting out problems.	"they're bad, like what I did" "never let 'em out they kill people"
#8 Why should women and children be saved first in a shipwreck?	Sex difference and sexual role themes. Danger themes, punishment themes, child vs. adult roles, confusion and difficulty.	"women are more important than men" "men more capable" "women better"

#9 Why is it better to pay bills by check than by cash?

Guilt feelings, emphasis on spending, buy-now-pay-later orientation, parental arguments over money.

"you'd be blamed for stealing it"
"don't have to pay any money"
"get what you want"
"daddy would be mad again"

#10 Why is it generally better to give money to an organized charity than to a street beggar?

Preoccupation with dissipation. Preoccupation with exploitation.

"beggar get drunk"
"he'd be real rich, have a million dollars"

#11 Why should most government positions be filled through examinations?

Concern over Communism and infiltration. Concern over health.

"catch spies"
"find if he has cancer"

#12 Why is cotton fiber used in making cloth?

Concern over expense. Concern over cleanliness.

"cheap"
"wash out germs"
"so never be dirty—smell bad"

#13 Why do we elect senators and congress-men?

Preoccupation with exploitation.

"so not have a Hitler"

14 Why should a promise be kept?

Exploitation, guilt.

"so they'd loan you something"
"it's a sin not to"

Item Composition and Difficulty

This part of the test employs items in question form and includes both practical problems and problems utilizing knowledge obtained from a more formal educational setting, such as the public school. Items as, "What is the thing to do when you cut your finger?" and "What is the thing to do if you lost one of your friend's balls?" are examples of the problems coming from everyday experience. These items call for clear one-reason responses and are primarily included to test the common sense conceptualizations of the very young child. Item #11 (government examination) and Item #13 (senators) are examples of items which depend highly upon the utilization of knowledge received in a public school setting and/or a particular socio-cultural setting. This will tend to unduly penalize bright young children who have not yet had the opportunity to acquire such knowledge from a formal educational setting. After the first five items, two clear-cut reasons are required for the subject to obtain full credit for his response. As is true for all other subtests of the WISC, the level of success which the child reaches on these items is not only dependent upon common everyday experience and/or school attendance but also depends to a very high degree upon the age of the child. At 7½ years of age the average child will achieve a raw score of eight. Typically, this is achieved by a score of two on the first four items, which means the child will have given one adequate common sense reason to each one of these items through item #4 (fight). Another typical pattern of successes at this age level involves giving responses that are at the full credit level for the first two items and responses which are given partial credit on items #3 through #6 (house-brick).

The average raw score of the child at 10½ years is twelve. This score may be obtained either by giving full credit responses on the first six items or, more commonly, full credit responses on the first four items and partial credit responses on the items five through eight (women-children). By 13½ years the average child will achieve a raw score of 16 and typically this score is obtained by scoring scattered successes throughout the entire range of items (Chart II).

Correct serial placement of items in terms of ascending order of difficulty is another area of concern for all those individuals using the WISC.

As with Information, Sutherland (1960) analyzed item placement with normal referred children. While he found that Item #4 (fight) should have been placed before Item #3 (loaf-bread), it would appear that for normal children serial placement of the items in the original format is basically satisfactory.

With a retarded sample (MA 8), Carleton and Stacey (1955) found item difficulty was the same as with the normal sample, although Item #6 (house-brick) was slightly easier than Item #5 (train-track). From Item #7 (criminals) on, the subjects were unable to achieve one or two point scores because the items were beyond them—in this case placement of the later items had no significance since all were failed.

Significant Differences between Comprehension and Other Subtests

Hopkins and Michael (1961), in their analyses of significant differences between Comprehension and the other subtests, found that when Comprehension is paired with Arithmetic, Vocabulary or Block Design there must be a difference of at least four weighted score points to obtain a statistically significant difference at the five per cent level. For a significant difference to appear between Comprehension and any of the other subtests, a difference of five points or more was required.

Factorial Age Variables

When the WISC standardization data is factor analyzed (Cohen 1959), Comprehension proves to be a moderately good measure of general intelligence (Spearman's G), although it is surpassed by the other "essentially verbal" subtests (Information, Similarities and Vocabulary). It is limited in value by being the least reliable of any subtest in this group.

At the earlier age levels a factor hypothesized as reflecting "the application of judgment to situations following some implicit verbal manipulation" (Verbal Comprehension II) is apparent, but this decreases with age. However, by 13½ years of age, another factor, "verbally retained knowledge impressed by formal education" (Verbal Comprehension I), contributes substantially for the first time. Thus, Comprehension seems to decline through the years as a measure of judgment, as the formally over-learned "right" answers are increasingly available to the child.

There is very little evidence in the analysis which can be attributed to a specific factor of "Comprehension." Also there is much more variability due to unreliability of the subtest. Therefore, in clinical practice it is not recommended that Comprehension scores *in themselves* generally be interpreted as measuring either verbal judgment, knowledge, or comprehension. In other words, this subtest's utility is achieved by its combination with other subtests to measure verbal facility and general intelligence. It would seem that success or failure here should be examined carefully for chance factors before any specific interpretation is attempted.

Using Guilford and Merrifield's Structure-of-Intellect components, the Comprehension items themselves have been categorized under three factors. The initial items, #1 through #5, are considered to call for Judgment: to choose the best change of emphasis or interpretation in terms of an idea or set of ideas or meanings (there is no empirical evidence for this factor as yet). Items #6 and #7 are listed under the above but also under Verbal Comprehension: to know the meanings conventionally attached to words in a language. Items #8 through #14 are classified under Sensitivity to Problems: to explicate, in some detail, the best description of one's uncertainty in a semantic situation (Chart II).

The judgment and verbal comprehension factors attributed to the earlier items tend to agree with Cohen's factors. The change of interpretation at item #8 to Sensitivity to Problems is consistent at least with Cohen's minimization of judgment as a factor for older children, since these items are typically administered to children over ten years of age.

Advantages

Probably the chief advantage of this subtest lies in the fact that it is a rich mine of clinically relevant material. This ranges from outright bizarre thinking or extreme preoccupation with self or specific themes on the one hand to compulsive, perfectionistic doubting or ambivalence on the other.

Peculiar habits of verbalization can be noted, as well as perverse or anti-social reactions (i.e., "I wouldn't do anything!"). Limited education, by the middle years, is not particularly penalizing, since most children by that time are exposed to the required information. The test indicates how well the child has overlearned conventional social knowledge. A sudden poor response embedded in a setting of excessively stereotyped, parroted answers is indicative of a gap in judgment and hence pathology. Comprehension items are relatively easy to answer, so that virtually all children experience some success here. This subtest gives some knowledge of the child's coping ability as well as his interest in coping.

At the lower end of the scale, Comprehension also allows a comparison between school-acquired knowledge and knowledge that can be picked up in the everyday world of experience.

Limitations

One very important disadvantage of Comprehension lies in the requirement for multiple responses on the later items, a requirement which can hardly be inferred by the child. This can be penalizing for two types of children: the child who strives to give the single "best" response, and the child who is simply not compulsive and feels (not without reason) that one answer is sufficient.

Younger children must be independent and oriented toward problem-solving to attempt an answer to items covering situations they have never heard of. Even very bright young children are not exposed to many of the Comprehension items. On the other hand, older children may do well simply because they have learned to reel off rules of behavior without necessarily understanding them. Further, Comprehension can penalize creative individuals searching for unusual solutions to problems.

This test is particularly vulnerable to maladjustment, more than any other subtest. Thus, items which prove to be traumatic may confuse intellectual evaluation, since transient emotional reactions become the governing factor, rather than cognitive functioning. Dependency needs and their correlative factor, maternal overprotection, can greatly limit success.

Summary of Interpretations

Specific responses often give rich clinical cues about the child's preoccupations and his ability to cope with them. They may indicate a passive, infantile child, an impulsive, hostile child, a guilt-ridden child, or a seriously disturbed, bizarre child who displays atypical affect. Any of these children will have difficulty coping with everyday life; Comprehension may reveal how these difficulties manifest themselves.

High scores may indicate a number of factors: canny, practical qualities, wide experience, superior organization of knowledge, social maturity, ability to verbalize well. A drive toward productivity (multiple responses) can indicate compulsive trends or simply a high level of aspiration.

Low scores, on the other hand, can suggest a number of meanings. For one, the child's ability to cope with his everyday environment may have been limited due to restrictions of a physical or psychological nature. With respect to the latter, such factors as over-dependency come to mind as typical of the emotional factors which affect cognitive processes. For another, overly concrete thinking limits the capacity to accept hypothetical premises and work out hypothetical conclusions. Some non-verbal children simply do not say enough to reach a satisfactory level (especially bilingual children). Some children have little experience in making their ideas explicit in words. Others, who are too perfectionistic, may spoil answers by adding unnecessary additions or specifications. Finally one must consider the presence of phobic thoughts arising from certain items (i.e., "cut finger," "train wreck").

ARITHMETIC SUBTEST

Description and History

This section of the WISC includes 16 timed problems, of which the first three, involving blocks, are given only to children below the age of 8 or to older suspected mental defectives. The last three items are presented to the subject on separate cards and are to be read aloud.

Arithmetic problems are designed to measure mental alertness by checking the child's ability to reason using simple numerical operations which are readily available to children in our society. In the history of the development of intelligence tests, items of this type were utilized by the original Binet-Simon Test of Intelligence Scales. A little later such items were included on the Kuhlmann-Anderson (1927), which is essentially a group test of intelligence. From this initial usage of items concerned with numerical calculations, it has been found that such problems correlate significantly with total scores of intelligence scales, avoid verbalization and reading difficulties, and have high predictive value in respect to potential mental ability. Consequently, subsequent revisions of the Binet-type tests as well as group tests such as California Test of Mental Maturity (1957) have utilized this type of item. With evidence of such high predictive value of mental abilities, Wechsler included this type of question on both his adult and child scales.

Rationale

This subtest is based on the concept that ability to manipulate number concepts is one criterion of intelligence. This idea, in turn, is derived from repeated observation that the richness of a culture is directly related to the use of number concepts by its members; presumably the richer the culture, the more intelligent the people. One facet of this manipulation is mental alertness or concentration. The arithmetic problems require a directed focusing of concentration, an extracting of the relations involved. To do this, the subject must understand and attend to the pattern of the four basic numerical operations (addition, subtraction, division, and multiplication) as well as the abstract continuum of numbers. Another assumption which this subtest makes is that the elementary knowledge required by these items is acquired and becomes internalized in the course of ordinary life experiences. Basically, however, as with Information, this kind of knowledge is primarily taught in the public school system.

The problem becomes a process of focused concentration, which is even more emphasized by the time limits on each item. With time pressures, the subject is focused to apply himself actively to the problem. Children with higher mental capacities will presumably be able to turn to internalized patterns of numerical functions in order to solve a problem presented to them.

What the Test Measures

This subtest of the WISC requires meaningful manipulation of complex thought patterns. It is a measure of the child's ability to utilize abstract concepts of number and numerical operations, which are measures of cognitive development. Since concentration and attention are non-cognitive functions in essence, and manipulation of number operations is cognitive, this test is of value in that it furnishes a demonstration of how the child relates cognitive and non-cognitive factors in terms of thinking and performance.

The child must demonstrate on this subtest the ability to translate word problems into arithmetic operations. Occasionally, this subtest can be a measure of deviant thinking processes, particularly with the more difficult items. However, except for certain subjects for whom the word "arithmetic" is significant as a negatively conditioned response, the content of this subtest is not perceived as traumatic. Further, bizarre content responses are rarely observed here.

CHART III. ARITHMETIC SUBTEST

Guilford factors for all items

General reasoning
Symbol facility

Item placement of average scores for three age levels

Age 7½ (average raw score 5-6) success through items 5 or 6
Age 10½ (average raw score 9) success through item 9
Age 13½ (average raw score 12) success through item 12

3. ARITHMETIC				
Problem		Response	Time	Score 1 or 0
1. 45"	9 blocks +			
2. 45"	4 blocks —			
3. 45"	7 blocks —			
4. 30"	apple ÷			
5. 30"	pennies +			
6. 30"	marbles +			
7. 30"	newspapers —			
8. 30"	cigars ×			
9. 30"	milk bottles —			
10. 30"	pennies ÷			
11. 30"	workman ÷			
12. 60"	oranges ×, —			
13. 30"	number ÷, ×			
14. 60"	pencils ÷, ×			
15. 120"	taxi —, ×, +			
16. 120"	card game ÷, —			

Item Composition and Difficulty

This subtest includes items utilizing the four basic arithmetic operations: addition, subtraction, multiplication, and division. Fifteen items involve simple numerical skills and the sixteenth adds to this an exercise in logic. Basically these items utilize knowledge obtained from both practical and formal educational settings. Items #1, #2, and #3, blocks added and subtracted manually, are examples of problems coming from a practical, concrete setting, whereas items #6

(8 marbles and 6 marbles) and #7 (12 newspapers less 5), are usually gleaned from a more formal setting such as the public school.

As with the other verbal tests on this scale, the level of success on Arithmetic is not only dependent upon common everyday experience and knowledge obtained from a school setting but also upon the age of the child. By 7½ years of age a raw score of 5 or 6 is expected from the average child (this would include #5, 4 pennies and 2 pennies, and #6, 8 marbles and 6 marbles) while a raw score of 9 is average for the 10½ year old child (this would include #9, 25 bottles less 11). These items call for simple addition, subtraction, multiplication and division operations which are easily transferred by children in these age groups from their school experiences. Between 10½ and 13½ there seems to be little increase in arithmetic skills. The child by 13½ years is expected to average a raw score of 12, which means that he is expected to perform not only the basic operations of the four elementary computational processes but also be able to work one problem (#12, 3 dozen oranges) where more than one basic arithmetical process is operating. It should be recalled that this subtest places a high premium on mental alertness or concentration and that high powered mathematical knowledge is not required to pass the items (Chart III).

As mentioned in discussing the other subtests, placement of items in this subtest has been analyzed by Sutherland (1960). Only one question is misplaced with respect to ascending order of difficulty—#10 (72 divided by 4) is considerably harder than #11 (36 divided by 4) and #12 ($1 minus 3 times .30). In their mentally retarded sample with a mental age of 8, Carleton and Stacey (1955) found ¾ of their subjects answered the first five items (including #5, 4 pennies plus 2 pennies) correctly, but from that point on there was a very rapid dropoff, and evidence of only minimal discriminative ability. As can be seen, however, this agrees with expectations for the age 7½ years. From these results it would appear that here too more items are needed to discriminate among the different levels of the mentally retarded and borderline children.

Statistically Significant Differences between Arithmetic and Other Subtests

Hopkins and Michael (1961), in their analysis of significant differences between Arithmetic and any other WISC subtest, suggests that to differentiate at the five per cent level between the Arithmetic score and the Vocabulary score there must be at least 3 weighted points of difference. For the same differentiation involving Information, Comprehension, Similarities, Picture Arrangement, and Block Design this must rise to four points. For the remaining subtests, a difference of five points was found to be required.

Factorial Age Variables

The factor analysis of the WISC made by Cohen (1959) revealed that Arithmetic is similar to Comprehension as a measure of general intelligence (G). At $7\frac{1}{2}$ and $10\frac{1}{2}$ this subtest is contributing something to Verbal Comprehension I or "verbally retained knowledge impressed by formal education." This factor, of course, subsumes knowledge of counting skills, that is, basic numerical operations. Cohen found that by age $13\frac{1}{2}$, Arithmetic measures specifically "freedom from distractability," particularly when combined with Digit Span. It should be pointed out however that Cohen found this test to be highly unreliable and that much of the observed differences among children are due to chance factors.

Because of the high degree of unreliability, neither of the above factors nor the degree of arithmetic skills should be estimated from this subtest. However, at $10\frac{1}{2}$ and $13\frac{1}{2}$ large differences would allow one to draw inferences of specific Arithmetic ability or disability. Otherwise the testor should turn to another test particularly designed for this purpose.

From this evidence it would seem that Arithmetic may serve for the younger child as a measure of a kind of verbal intelligence. However, by the time a child has reached his teens it appears that this test is more related to attention based on manipulation of numerical operations.

Using Guilford and Merrifield's Structure-of-Intellect components (Chart III), the Arithmetic items are all classified under the same two factors—General Reasoning: To comprehend the nature of basic relationships in a problem preparatory to solving it; and Symbolic Facility (including numerical facility): To recall rapidly expected results of stated actions on signs, numbers, and code elements. Both of these seem to be variants of Cohen's Verbal Comprehension. Interestingly, the Freedom from Distractability factor does not seem to be covered, except perhaps indirectly as related to rapid recall.

Advantages

A rapid estimate of number skills and skill with word problems can be adjudged. No advanced calculations are required by any of the problems. Attitudes toward learning and classroom successes and failures can be inferred from behavior and comments (as example, a poignant, "I'm no good at this, I'm the worst in the room").

Limitations

The item range for any one individual may be insufficient. The test is very susceptible to the effects of anxiety. Finally, #10, the 72 pennies item is too difficult for its placement in the series.

Summary of Interpretations

Arithmetic is more likely than some of the other subtests to reveal important clues to personality and attitudes toward school achievement. For instance, the authority dominated youngster who is eager to please may do quite well while the resistant child who refuses even to try may do very poorly.

A high score may indicate an obedient, teacher-oriented student. It can also indicate good concentration on the part of the child. Since success on #16 cannot be achieved without superior intelligence, this one item can be highly diagnostic of unusual intellectual ability.

A low score can indicate poor attention and distractability caused by anxiety invading the thinking processes. It may also demonstrate poor school achievement perhaps due to rebellion against authority or cultural disadvantage. Transient emotional reactions can cause marked variation in this subtest; for example, a child worried about his parents' battle the night before may do very poorly the next day on this one subtest.

Very low scores, save in the case of the mentally retarded, suggest serious emotional disturbance and possible loss of reality ties, since the easiest items are distinctly overlearned and hard to miss.

SIMILARITIES SUBTEST

Description and History

This part of the test consists of a simple initial section involving four incomplete sentences calling for previously learned associations and given only to children below the age of eight or to older suspected mental defectives, and twelve pairs of words requiring the identification of likenesses, essential or superficial, between objects, substances, facts, or ideas.

Originally this type of item was used sparingly on the Binet-Simon Scales and subsequently on all further revisions of that scale. However, so many individuals failed this type of item that Wechsler in developing his initial scale almost omitted it altogether. For example, average adults failed the item on the Binet asking for the similarity between evolution and revolution. Wechsler (1944) consequently was inclined to doubt the wisdom of including such items on his scale for he initially believed it was impossible to devise a similarities test that would be free of linguistic difficulties. After concluding an initial investigation, however, he discovered that it was possible to increase serially the difficulty of the items without resorting to strange and unusual words. Since Similarities historically had been demonstrated as an excellent test of general intelligence, Wechsler therefore included it on both adult and child scales.

Rationale

All people make implicit use of classificatory relationships in their continuing attempt to adjust to environmental, interpersonal, and intrapersonal events. Explicit elaboration of such schemes is thought to be one measure of intelligence. The range of an individual's ability to discriminate likenesses is thought to correlate with general intelligence. The more intelligent a person is, the broader will be his interests. He will have more creativity and imagination, and therefore be able to discern essential relationships to a greater degree. Classificatory relationships develop in the child through exposure to materials and information both at home and at school.

What the Test Measures

This part of the WISC is basically constructed to determine the qualitative aspects of relationships which the subject has abstracted from his environment. The subject has obtained facts and ideas from his surroundings and should be able to see basic, essential relationships between them. The test calls into operation remote memory, ability to comprehend, capacity for associative thinking, interests and reading patterns of the subject, as well as the ability to select and verbalize appropriate relationships between two ostensibly dissimilar objects or concepts. These are then reduced to measures ordering into hierarchical classes essential versus superficial likenesses (e.g., the essential similarity of plum and peach is that they are both fruits rather than they are both round). Lower order and higher order abstractions are also shown by performance on these items (e.g., a lower order abstraction of the similarity between beer and wine is that they both are to drink whereas the higher form of abstraction is that both are alcoholic beverages).

Item Composition and Difficulty

Similarities includes four items which almost all children learn about in their everyday experience. These four items call for the subject to use associative thinking processes. An example of such items is #1, "Lemons are sour and sugar is _____?" The remaining twelve items on this subtest are concerned with essential and non-essential likenesses. These items call for the child to use his reasoning or concept formation ability; #5, "In what way are a plum and a peach alike?", #10, "In what way are a pound and a yard alike?" and #15, "In what way are first and last alike?" are examples of items which involve the child's ability to reason in a logical manner.

Results of the younger child are dependent upon the amount of learning and exposure to facts and general information which he has had. The results for older children are often unduly influenced by knowledge of material which they have over-learned rather than by conceptualizing skills.

Each item in this subtest can be scored to distinguish between superficial and superior responses. There is an obvious difference both as to maturity and as to level of thinking between the child who says that a plum and a peach are alike because they have skins and the child who says they are both fruit. When the child says a peach and plum are alike because they both have skins or because you can eat them he receives a credit of one, indicating a superficial answer. When the child responds they are both fruit he receives a credit of two, indicating that he has given an answer involving the essential aspect of the link between them. He consequently receives greater credit for a superior answer. This qualitative difference in response is of value not only because it furnishes a discriminative scoring method, but also because it is often very suggestive of the evenness and level of the subject's intellectual functioning. Some subjects' total scores, even when relatively good, are largely made up of 1 answer, whereas the scores of others are of an unpredictable proportion of 0, 1 and 2 credits. The former are most likely to be of mediocre caliber, of a type from which high level intellectual functioning may not be expected; the latter, while uneven and erratic, have many more potentialities and possibilities.

Developmental age patterns of these items are also found for this subtest. The average raw score for age 7½ years is 6. Usually this is attained by passing the first four items plus one or two reasoning items beyond, depending on the level of the subject's abstraction.

4. SIMILARITIES	Score 1 or 0
1. Lemons—Sugar	
2. Walk—Throw	
3. Boys—Girls	
4. Knife—Glass	
5. Plum—Peach	Score 2, 1 or 0
6. Cat—Mouse	
7. Beer—Wine	
8. Piano—Violin	
9. Paper—Coal	

10. Pound—Yard	
11. Scissors—Copper Pan	
12. Mountain—Lake	
13. Salt—Water	
14. Liberty—Justice	
15. First—Last	
16. 49—121	

CHART IV. SIMILARITIES SUBTEST

Guilford factors

Items 1-4   Associational fluency
Items 5-16   Semantic relations
             Expressional fluency

Item placement of average scores for three age levels

Age 7½ (average raw score 6) success on item 5 or above
Age 10½ (average raw score 9) success on item 7 or above
Age 13½ (average raw score 13) success on item 9 or above

This means including (depending on scatter) item #5, "In what way are a plum and a peach alike?" By 10½ years of age the average child is expected to attain a raw score of 9 including item #7, "In what way are beer and wine like?"—again depending on the quality of the answer. The average child of 13½ years is expected to make a raw score of 13 which includes answers to or beyond item #9, "In what way are paper and coal alike?" once more depending upon the child's level of understanding abstract relationships (Chart IV).

Particular placement of each item on this subtest was analyzed by Sutherland (1960). In his sample of referred children ranging in age from 7 through 15, he did not find significant differences from the standardization placement, although item #5, "In what way are a plum and a peach alike?" and item #6, "In what way are a cat and mouse alike?" reversed positions. This was equally true of item #7, "In what way are beer and wine alike?" and item #8, "In what way are a piano and a violin alike?" He also noted a tendency for item #10, "In what way are pound and yard alike?" and item #11, "In what way are scissors and copper pan alike?" to receive a credit of either two or none.

Evidence of item placement according to difficulty was also studied by Carlton and Stacey (1955) for a sample of retarded children with a mental age of eight. In this sample of children, 84 per cent or more passed the first three items whereas item #4, "A knife and a piece of glass both _____?" and item #5, "In what way are a plum and peach alike?" were reversed in difficulty. Item #8, "In what way are a piano and a violin alike?" was much easier for these children than the two preceding items. Beyond item #8, however, few responses of these subjects met either of the criteria of essential or superficial likenesses. As in the Information and Arithmetic subtests it probably would be of value to add more items of a medium level of difficulty to help discriminate the upper levels of retarded children as well as the lower levels of borderline children.

Some of the items may trigger emotion-laden responses, although less commonly than on Comprehension. Often valuable diagnostic cues can be derived from a study of the child's responses as related to the appropriateness and level of his active conceptual thinking. For example, the item concerned with the similarity between knife and glass may bring associations of injury, particularly that resulting from disobedience. The cat and mouse item can trigger an association of injury as well as aggression or persecution. The beer-wine item may give a surprisingly graphic picture of parental activities and children's reactions to parental drunkenness and lack of control.

There are other implications for screening children in the Similarities subtest. Experience shows that there are at least three levels of content which the subject can use in answering Similarity items, namely the concrete, the functional, and the abstract. On the concrete level of concept formation, either a specific common feature of the things in question is considered to be the content linking them (a peach and a plum are alike because they have skins), or the content linking them is concrete (beer and wine are found in bottles). On the functional level, the child sees the function of the two things (plum and peach can both be eaten). On the abstract level, a general term is given which sums up all the essential characteristics of the two objects (plum and peach are both fruits).

The conceptual content of the first two levels is too limited and does not include all the essential content for both things, whereas the last level in contrast does subsume the ideas of the other levels and adds all the essential qualities linking the two words together with a general term.

The non-achieving child who receives a high score may be using fantasy abstractions in contrast to the here and now type of concrete relations which make up much of the work in the school. Obsessive children probably will do very well on this subtest since credit is given for the higher level abstraction if there is more than one response. Low scores probably will indicate children, and particularly older children, who have an overly concrete approach, rigidity of thought processes ("They are not alike"), and serious distortion of thought processes ("Pound is to beat up and that is what I do whenever anybody comes into our yard"). Finally low scores can indicate profound distrust ("You are trying to fool me—they are not alike").

Significant Differences Between Similarities and Other Subtests

In order to obtain a statistical significant difference at the five per cent level between the Similarities subtest and any other subtest, wide differences must exist. For the Information, Arithmetic, Vocabulary, and Block Design subtests, there must be at least a difference of four weighted score points to obtain a significant difference at the five per cent level (Hopkins and Michael, 1961). Hopkins and Michael also found that a difference of five weighted score points is required to yield statistical significance at the five per cent level between Similarities and any one of the other remaining subtests.

Factorial Age Variables

When Cohen (1959) factor analyzed the WISC he found the Similarities scores to be an important component of the WISC. It proved to a moderately good measure of general intelligence (Spearman's G) in children. At the younger ages ($7\frac{1}{2}$ and $10\frac{1}{2}$) it appears to measure Verbal Comprehension I, "verbally retained knowledge impressed by formal education," while at the older age level, $13\frac{1}{2}$, it measures both the former as well as Verbal Comprehension II, "application of judgment to situations following some implicit verbal manipulation." However, chance factors are likely to have strong influence upon Similarities scores. It is therefore unjustified for clinical interpretation to stress either or both of these factors. Similarly, a purely mechanical interpretation of the Similarities items as representing abstract thinking is unjustified.

Using the Guilford and Merrifield Structure of Intellect components, the first four Similarity items are classified under a single factor: Associational Fluency: To produce many relations having a given idea in common. The advanced items (#5 through #16), which begin the test for children eight and older, are classified under two factors: Semantic Relations: To comprehend relationships between ideas; and Expressional Fluency: To produce many sets of inter-related ideas (Chart IV).

Compared with Cohen's factor analysis, the above factors appear to show less direct relationship to the Verbal Comprehension factors he proposed than was observed on the previous subtests. While comprehension is mentioned in the first, the emphasis appears to be on the ability to come up with a variety of ideas—this in contrast to a "one right answer" approach.

Advantages

Similarities provides a rough measure of the ability to abstract by means of verbalization, which, however, may be quite terse and still satisfactory. There is a good range of items and the test takes little time to administer. Personal preoccupations can be determined by specific responses to certain items.

Limitations

The gap between simple completion items (#1 to #4) and abstraction items (#5 on) is too large. Particularly for the younger child, the scale is too compressed. Also, successes are often a result of memory, experience or coaching rather than original concept formation.

Summary of Interpretations

There are numerous implications for screening children in Similarities. Susceptibility to fear and guilt have been mentioned previously. Too, Similarities may detect the extremely concrete child who cannot grasp the concepts required or is limited to superficial concepts.

High scores sometimes suggest the non-achiever who prefers fantasy abstractions to the "here-and-now" which makes up much of school work. The level of concept formation achieved is important —the more abstract the response, the higher the level of intelligence. A trichotomy which has proved helpful is that of the concrete, the functional, and abstract or conceptual. Exemplifying this would be the plum-peach item: concrete level, "they have skins," functional level, "they can be eaten," higher order abstraction, "they are fruit." This last subsumes the earlier ideas (skins and eating) and adds an additional one. Obsessive children may do well in this test, since additional credit may be earned by giving more than one reason, and in the process achieving a higher level of abstraction.

Low scores serve to indicate an overly concrete mode of approach (particularly notable in older children), rigidity of thought processes or negativism ("they aren't alike!"), and, most seriously, distortion of thought processes as shown by atypical concept formations (i.e., "Pound is to beat up and that's what I do whenever anybody comes into our yard"). Finally, low scores can indicate distrust ("You're tricking me—they're different!").

VOCABULARY SUBTEST

Description and History

This subtest of the WISC is composed of forty words to be defined, presenting in ascending order of difficulty. The first nine are presented only to children below the age of eight or to older suspected mental defectives. The type of item included requires a knowledge of words generally available to children within our society. This type of item has been used in measuring intelligence on an individual basis since the original Binet-Simon scales appeared early in the twentieth century. Subsequently, group intelligence tests have also included vocabulary sections. Word definitions, then, have been a standard measure of general intelligence since the introduction of mental tests, primarily because the extent of a person's store of words has proved to be an excellent means to demonstrate his fund of general verbal information.

Rationale

Definition of words implies the reorganization of ideas through an implicit manipulation of verbal signs and symbols and, as such, has long been considered one criterion of intelligence. In tests such as the WISC which depend on normative standards, the factors of home background and educational opportunity can contribute importantly to the score. Vocabulary is assumed to be a measure of learning ability, of verbal information and range of ideas influenced by a child's educational background and his cultural setting.

What the Test Measures

This subtest is probably the best single measure of general intellectual level. It gives an excellent picture of the child's learning ability, fund of information, richness of ideas, kind and quality of language, degree of abstract thinking, and character of thought processes. Vocabulary reflects a child's level of education and environment. As seen by Wechsler (1958), Vocabulary is often of value because of its qualitative aspects. There is an obvious difference between a child who defines "donkey" as "an animal" and a child who says, "a four legged beast of burden classified with the mammals." Obviously, this gives the examiner an excellent chance to examine the subject's richness of ideas, his quality and kind of language, as well as his degree of abstract thinking. It should be noted that the quality and kind of language sometimes tells the examiner something about the child's social and cultural milieu. The types of words which a child fails and passes also is of significance. For example, dull subjects from educated homes may pass uncommon words such as #21, "shilling," and #24, "espionage," but fail much easier ones. From the clinical point of view, the most important feature of verbal definitions is the semantic character of a definition which gives insight into the nature of the child's thought processes. This is particularly true of children who are not oriented to reality; their use of language often is diagnostic (#13, "sword"—"is a dinasword!").

Item Composition and Difficulty

This subtest consists of forty words which theoretically are arranged in the order of ascending difficulty. The first five items are scored either two or zero, which means if the child gets the item at all he is given full credit for it. This naturally limits the discrimination of the scale at an early age. The remaining thirty-five terms are scored at three levels, depending on the quality of the response. A child is given a score of 2 for the correct abstract answer, a score of 1 for the correct concrete answer, and zero for an incorrect or irrelevant answer. Older children are not given the first nine items,

	Score 2 or 0	5. VOCABULARY
1. Bicycle		
2. Knife		
3. Hat		
4. Letter		
5. Umbrella		
	Score 2, 1 or 0	
6. Cushion		
7. Nail		
8. Donkey		
9. Fur		
10. Diamond		
11. Join		
12. Spade		
13. Sword		
14. Nuisance		
15. Brave		
16. Nonsense		
17. Hero		
18. Gamble		
19. Nitroglycerine		
20. Microscope		
21. Shilling		
22. Fable		
23. Belfry		
24. Espionage		
25. Stanza		
26. Seclude		
27. Spangle		
28. Hara-Kiri		
29. Recede		
30. Affliction		
31. Ballast		
32. Catacomb		
33. Imminent		
34. Mantis		
35. Vesper		
36. Aseptic		
37. Chattel		
38. Dilatory		
39. Flout		
40. Traduce		

CHART V. VOCABULARY SUBTEST

Guilford factor for all items

Verbal comprehension

Item placement of average scores for three age levels

Age 7½ (average raw score 21-22) success on item 10 and above
Age 10½ (average raw score 31-33) success on item 16 and above
Age 13½ (average raw score 42-44) success on item 21 and above

being credited for them if they succeed on item #10, "diamond" on, based on the assumption that these simple words are over-learned material for them.

Results are dependent on the age of the child, socio-economic status, the amount of exposure to facts and general information which the child has had. The amount of formal schooling influences the child's level of defining words. A child's native language would also be an important factor in his ability to define words in the English language.

Each item on this subtest can be scored to distinguish between superficial or concrete responses, and superior or abstract responses. There are obvious qualitative differences between the thinking of a child who defines diamond as "jewelry" and a child who defines it as "the hardest known most expensive mineral used to cut all other minerals." The first response is scored *one* indicating a concrete superficial answer whereas the latter answer is scored *two* indicating that the more abstract connotative qualities of the word have been given. The qualitative differences in response are of value because they allow a refined scoring method to be used. Also two point responses are suggestive of the high level of thinking employed.

At age 7½ the average child achieves a raw score of 21-22, typically indicating all or partial credit is achieved on item #11, "join," and beyond. At 10½, a raw score of 32-33 is average, with the subject achieving some success beyond item #16, "nonsense." For age 13½, a raw score of 43-44 is average, which means success beyond #21, "hero" (Chart V).

Sex differences noted by Jastak and Jastak (1964) suggest that #13, "sword," #14, "nuisance," #18, "gamble," #19, "nitroglycerine," and #31, "ballast," are easier for boys and that #3, "hat," #10, "diamond," and #27, "spangle," are easier for girls.

Certain words have potential clinical significance, for example, "sword" and "brave." The words "nuisance" ("what I am") or "nonsense" ("you say something to your father") are other examples of words eliciting emotion-laden response.

Sutherland (1960) found that for average "referred" children some words were considerably misplaced with respect to relative difficulty. The following placement was found to be more accurate, in terms of ascending order of difficulty: #7, 8, 13, 6, 9, 10, 11, 15, 17, 12, 14, 18, 20, 19, 21. Thus #13, "sword," for example, is much easier than original placement indicated, and #12, "spade," is far more difficult. Sutherland also found a rather abrupt increase in difficulty by #22, "fable," and #23, "belfry."

Carlton and Stacey (1955) found the first eight items were readily passed by 80 percent of a mentally retarded sample (MA 8), with the exception of #4, "letter," which proved to be more difficult. After #15, "brave," discrimination was slight although #18, "gamble," proved to be unexpectedly easy.

Significant Differences between Vocabulary and Other Subtests

Hopkins and Michael (1961) suggest that a significant difference (.05 level) between Vocabulary and other subtests must be at least 3 points when paired with Information, Comprehension, Similarities, Picture Completion, or Picture Arrangement. Differences of 5 points or more are required when paired with Digits, Object Assembly, or Coding.

Factorial Age Variables

More than any other subtest of the WISC, Vocabulary ranks as the single best indicator of intelligence (G). At age 7½ there is some evidence of Verbal Comprehension II—"application of judgment following implicit verbal manipulation." This shifts to Verbal Comprehension I or "verbal knowledge impressed by formal education" at ages 10½ and 13½. The factor analytic procedure did not come up with a specific factor for word knowledge. Vocabulary is essentially a measure of general intelligence, and specific interpretations are not usually justified.

Under the Structure-of-Intellect analysis, Vocabulary items are classified under a single factor, Verbal Comprehension: To know the meanings conventionally attached to words in a language (Chart V). This agrees with the Cohen analysis, although it does not differentiate between comprehension due to specific judgment and that attributable to education.

Advantages

This subtest is an excellent, speedy measure for assessing intellectual potential; it is considered the best single measure of intelligence. So long as the content is acceptable, awkward or poorly worded presentation of definitions is not penalized. Vocabulary is relatively invulnerable to emotional disturbance. Disturbed children who are intellectually capable do well on this test. At the same time the items give useful leads as to a child's preoccupation. Verbal fluency and cultural level are accurately measured by Vocabulary.

Limitations

Scoring is difficult because of subjectivity, and hence unreliability is a problem. In addition, scores may be invalid due to bilingualism or cultural disadvantage of some groups of children. Also, Vocabulary takes a long time to administer.

Summary of Interpretations

Content and manner of word definition often yield valuable clues to the child's background. For instance, sporadic high level successes interspersed with low-grade definitions of simpler words is characteristic of the dull or borderline child living in a home with cultural advantages including high educational level of parents.

Definitions studded with derogatory self-references ("I'm a nuisance") demonstrate the child's picture of himself and may indicate exposure to an unhealthy environment. Other words may give a vivid picture of family life, as in the case of a detailed description of forms of gambling.

High scores often indicate good familial-cultural background as well as good schooling. From this, subtest information is obtained of the range and richness of ideas, as well as level of abstract thinking in analyzing and synthesizing ideas. Thus, a florid wordiness suggests the mechanism of "intellectualization."

Many possibilities are suggested by low scores, chief among which are those of limited educational or familial background. In the case of certain minority groups, for example, children may not have been encouraged to express themselves verbally. This point is sometimes clarified by administering a picture vocabulary test where the child can point to the correct picture rather than put his answer in words. A marked difference between the two scores indicates the extent to which difficulty in verbalizing rather than ignorance limits vocabulary.

Emotional overtones are suggested by certain words, such as, #2, "knife," "you cut yourself bad—go to the hospital"; #14, "nuisance," "Your mother don't like you"; #15, "brave," "I'm not brave, I'm scared."

Aside from the score itself, severe emotional disturbance may be shown by a variety of signs of language and thought disturbance, such as the following: bizarre expressions as such a response to #9, "fur," as, "They have it at the circus. I have a lion—do you like the circus?"; clang associations such as hearing "cat" for #3, "hat," or "pail" for #7, "nail," and then defining the associated word; incoherent running together of words; perseverative giving of the same definition to successive words. These are all seen from time to time in the severely disturbed child.

PICTURE COMPLETION

Description and History

Picture Completion consists of 20 pictures, each of which has an important missing element. These pictures are to be named within a 15 second time limit and are arranged in an ascending order of difficulty.

During World War I, similar items were used in the Army Beta Scale (Yerkes, 1921). Such pictures also resemble the mutilated pictures of the original Binet.

Rationale

This test is founded on the premise that the ability to comprehend familiar objects visually and to determine the absence of essential rather than non-essential or irrelevant details is a valid measure of intelligence.

What the Test Measures

Picture Completion calls for visual identification of familiar objects, forms, and living things and the further capacity to identify and isolate essential from non-essential characteristics. Attention and concentration are important elements in the test.

Item Composition and Difficulty

The 20 items provide more of a range than found in some of the subtests, although the spread of scores for average children is not wide. At age 7½, children typically pass the first 8 items (#8, "card"). By age 10½, the first 11 items are achieved successfully (#11, "fish"). By early adolescence, at age 13½, an average child completes the first 13 items successfully (#13, "fly") (Chart VI).

There are some differences in response dependent on the sex of the testee. The #11, "fish," and #12, "screw," items are easier for boys, while the #15, "eyebrow," item is easier for girls. Traumatic material, that is, the sort of stimulus which could trigger an emotion-determined response, is generally absent from Picture Completion.

CHART VI. PICTURE COMPLETION SUBTEST

Guilford factors for all items

Visual or auditory cognition
Perceptual foresight
Figural relation selection*

Item placement of average scores for three age levels

Age 7½ (average raw score 8) success through
item 8

Age 10½ (average raw score 11) success
through item 11

Age 13½ (average raw score 13) success
through item 13)

* There is no empirical evidence for this factor as yet.

6. PICTURE COMPLETION	Score 1 or 0
1. Comb	
2. Table	
3. Fox	
4. Girl	
5. Cat	
6. Door	
7. Hand	
8. Card	
9. Scissors	
10. Coat	
11. Fish	
12. Screw	
13. Fly	
14. Rooster	
15. Profile	
16. Thermometer	
17. Hat	
18. Umbrella	
19. Cow	
20. House	

Any sort of affect-laden response would, therefore, be highly unusual and most significant, suggesting an intense problem.

Sutherland (1960) noted a number of changes in item placement. Thus, item #12, "screw," and #19, "cow," proved easier than their present placement would suggest, while #15, "profile," was more difficult.

Carleton and Stacey (1955) found the first 5 items and also #7 extremely easy for their mentally retarded sample (MA 8), with at least 84 per cent succeeding on each of these items. However from item #13 on failures were extremely common, with little discrimination possible. This indicates a good range of scores.

Significant Differences between Picture Completion and Other Subtests

Hopkins and Michael (1961) reported that significant differences (.05) between subtests required at least 4 weighted score points when Picture Completion is paired with other subtests, rising to 5 points or more when either Digits or Coding is involved.

Factorial Age Variables

Picture Completion is one of the poorer measures of general intelligence (G) in the WISC. Erratic successes and failures due to chance are particularly likely to occur on this task. The test appears to be contributing somewhat to Verbal Comprehension II, "the application of judgment to situation, following some implicit verbal manipulation." For children above age 10 it also measures Perceptual Organization, defined as "ability to interpret and organize visually perceived materials against a time limit." No individual or unique factor is measured and thus this test should not generally be interpreted in terms of a specific meaning.

Using the Guilford Structure-of-Intellect components, Picture Completion items are all classified under the same three factors: Visual or Auditory Cognition: To differentiate figural elements presented in an array; Perceptual Foresight: To be aware of possibilities implicit in a figural context; and Figural Relation Selection: To choose the figural relations best meeting a stated criterion (there is as yet no empirical evidence for this factor) (Chart VI).

There appears to be some relationship here to Cohen's Perceptual Organization, but otherwise there is little overlap between the Guilford and Merrifield and the Cohen factors.

Advantages

Picture Completion, which gives some estimate of the child's attention to the environment, is easy and quick to administer. It also has good face validity: that is, it appears intrinsically appealing to children. Picture Completion requires a minimum of verbalization, and is excellent for use with disturbed children when an "ice breaker" is required. It also provides a relaxation of tension for children who have found the verbal scale stressful. The range is excellent.

Picture Completion permits an examination of the child's susceptability to being led astray by unessential or irrelevant details, and to excessive projection.

Finally, Picture Completion is helpful in evaluating a child whose perception is adequate but whose ability to reproduce by visual-motor means (i.e., Block Designs) is poor.

Limitations

Despite the range of items, there seems to be relatively poor differentiation of scores in terms of increasing mental age.

The test is limited at the lower end of the age scale (true for most of the WISC, incidentally) because understanding the concept of "parts missing" is not established until the child has achieved a mental age of 6.

Test-taking "sets" are often established on this task. A negative set, leading to early failures, may be established. For example, some children reject item #8, "card," denying that they have ever seen cards. This probably explains the large measurement variance to some extent. The #13, "antenna," and #18, "umbrella," items are visually ambiguous for many otherwise bright children.

Summary of Interpretations

High scores may be due to any of several factors: ability to establish a learning set, excessive conformity ("not daring to miss a thing"), obsessive overattention to detail, compulsive perfectionism, and, finally, uncommonly good perception and concentration.

Low scores may lead to a hypothesis of other personality factors. Preoccupation with unessential details can be a sign of overt anxiety. Sometimes a poor score indicates pronounced negativism—"nothing is missing." The *need* to have nothing missing can also stem from concern over injury to the self. When the score is very low due to absurd aspects of the stimulus being named as missing, the adequacy of the subject's orientation to reality is called seriously into question.

Poor attention and concentration due to anxiety is probably the commonest source of low scores.

It is important to note the child's concern about his own accuracy. This can give important leads to the self concept and the ideal-self concept of the child. Does he note likely failures? Does he attempt to minimize the stigma of failure by stating that he cannot even recognize the object? This may represent a form of projection, attempting to put the blame on the picture and the "unfair" examiner. A more extreme form of projection occurs when the child "inserts" something into the picture which he then "removes"; for example, #10, "the man is missing fom the coat," #2, "the food is missing from the table." This also suggests excessive fluidity in thinking.

The child may also respond to difficulties in the task by finding fault with himself or with the picture. The former suggests a self-directed, guilt-ridden orientation; the latter, an other-directed, projecting orientation.

If the child misses grossly incomplete items while getting less obvious ones, something appears to be interfering with perception, causing it to be erratic or unstable. The presence of manifest anxiety can sometimes thus be inferred. When this tendency is pronounced, reality testing appears impaired and severe emotional problems are indicated.

PICTURE ARRANGEMENT

Description and History

This subtest consists of eleven different cut-up pictures, or picture sequences to be assembled, graded in order of difficulty. The first four are given to children below the age of eight or to older suspected mental defectives. Three of these are pictures in which the parts are put together as in simple jigsaw puzzles. The remaining eight are qualitatively different in that they consist of picture sequences, which when placed side by side in the proper order tell a logical story of actions or consequences. Time credits are given for speed of arrangement and there are time limits.

Apparently DeCroly first used a task of this sort as early as 1914. Other forms of the test were used in the Army Performance Scale of World War I and still later (1934) a series of such items was employed in the Cornell-Coxe Performance Scale.

Rationale

The ability to evaluate what is going on in a particular picture and to then place it logically in relation to other pictures so that a sensible and consistent story emerges is considered one criterion of intelligence.

What the Test Measures

Such factors as perception, visual compehension, planning involving sequential and causal events, and synthesis into intelligible wholes are involved in this test.

Performance on Picture Arrangement may indicate social alertness and common sense, as revealed in the application of so-called "social" intelligence, that is intelligence applied to social or interpersonal situations.

Item Composition and Difficulty

Picture Arrangement contains eleven items, four of which are administered only to children below the age of eight and to sus-

7. PICTURE ARRANGEMENT						
Arrangement	**Time**	**Order**	**Score**			
A. Dog 75"	1 — 2		0	1 ABC	2 ABC	
B. Mother 75"			0	1 OYT	2 TOY	
C. Train 60"			0	1 IR ON	2 IRON	
D. Scale 45"			0	2 ABC		
(Fight)						
1. Fire 45"			0	4 11-15 5 6-10 6 1-5 7 FIRE		
2. Burglar 45"			0	4 11-15 5 6-10 6 1-5 7 THUG		
3. Farmer 45"			0	4 11-15 5 6-10 6 1-5 7 QRST OR SQRT		
4. Picnic 45"			0	4 11-15 5 6-10 6 1-5 7 EFGH OR EFHG		
5. Sleeper 60"			0	4 16-20 5 11-15 6 1-10 7 PERCY		
6. Gardener 75"			0	4 21-30 5 16-20 6 1-15 7 FISHER OR FSIHER		
7. Rain 75"			0 2 MSTEAR ASTEMR	4 21-30 5 16-20 6 1-15 7 MASTER		

CHART VII. PICTURE ARRANGEMENT SUBTEST

Guilford factors for all items

Convergent production
Evaluation

Item placement of average scores for three age levels

Age 7½ (average raw score 14-16) success through item 2
Age 10½ (average raw score 27-28) success through item 4 or 5
Age 13½ (average raw score 31-33) success through item 5 or 6

pected mentally retarded children. Of these latter, three involve cut-up pictures; the remaining eight items and the example utilize sequences.

Age variables: At age 7½, a raw score of 14 to 16 is average, usually consisting of the first five items passed (A to D, plus #1, Fire, as a minimum) depending on time bonuses.

At age 10½, a raw score of 27 to 28 is average, usually consisting of items including #5, Sleeper, depending again on the extent of time bonuses. At age 13½, a raw score of 31 to 33 is average, usually beyond item #5 depending on time bonuses (Chart VII).

Certain items are potentially traumatic for younger children, especially when comic strip material is new to the child and not "extinguished" by over-exposure. Thus #1, Fire, may trigger preoccupations with themes of punishment and fire play; #2, Burgler, and #6, Gardner, may reflect concern over stealing and disobedience and #5, Sleeper, can be related to parental conflict.

Item difficulty as studied by Sutherland (1960) for average referred children ages 7 to 15 is essentially unchanged from the standardization format. However, item #5, Sleeper, did seem somewhat more difficult than the following two items, although not significantly so.

Carleton and Stacey (1955) reported the first three items (A-C) were passed by 87 per cent or more of a mentally retarded sample (MA 8) with a drastic drop in success from that point on. After #3, failures were commonplace.

Significant Differences between Picture Arrangement and Other Subtests

Hopkins and Michael (1961) reported that differences between subtests which reached the significant level (.05) were 4 points or more when Picture Arrangement was paired with Arithmetic, Vocabulary, or Block Design, but had to be at least 5 points when paired with Information, Comprehension, Similarities, Digits, Picture Completion, or Object Assembly, and 6 points when paired with Coding.

Factorial Age Variables

Picture Arrangement is the best single measure of general intelligence (G) among the performance scale tests, particularly at ages 7½ and 10½. When combined with Block Design it provides a good measure of non-verbal general intelligence. Care should be exercised in interpreting the results of this test too specifically, since chance variations in scores are considerable (Cohen, 1959).

On the Structure-of-Intellect components, all Picture Arrangement items are classified under two factors: Semantic Patterning: To generate from several given ideas a system in which they are interrelated in terms of their meanings; and Semantic Relation Selection: To select the relation most similar in meaning to a given or implied relation (Chart VII).

In Cohen's analysis, no specific factors were discovered for this subtest, and only its overall contribution to the measure of intelligence is mentioned.

Advantages

The comic strip format is attractive and the situation reasonably familiar to most children. Logical, sequential planning, rather than mere attentiveness as in Picture Completion, is stressed. This may, of course, be disrupted by emotional problems disclosed in the verbalizations accompanying the activity; information gained about the latter may be important in the overall evaluation of the child.

Limitations

Crucial to success is the presence or absence of typical life experiences, either actually experienced or seen in comic books or on television (for example, #2, Burglar).

The test is limited in that the concept of picture progression such as is needed here demands a mental age of approximately eight. Further, the first four items are really more like Object Assembly items than picture arrangements of the type seen in items #1-7 and are thus measuring something different. The range of the test is thus poor, being constricted by early difficulty and item change for the young child, and having a low ceiling for the older child.

Item #5, Sleeper, is poor in discriminative ability with failures almost totally due to the child ignoring the clock in the first two pictures. It poses a further liability in that failure here may impose an artificial top for the testee.

Summary of Interpretations

Picture Arrangement, as is true of Picture Completion, stresses perception of details, with the Picture Arrangement further providing a measure of the ability to manipulate these details logically.

Results of the subtest can be checked against Picture Completion and Block Design to differentiate purely perceptual defects from difficulties with organizing stimuli in sequential progression.

Observation of the manner of approach to the cards may throw light on the child's planning ability. Can he delay his solution until he looks over the situation carefully, and comes to a decision? Or does he utilize a less mature approach, proceeding piecemeal and quickly without verifying his predictions? Logical stories should be expected from the age of eight upward, while younger, less mature children may tend to see the pictures as separate elements. Matching elements from one picture to the next rather then judging the meaning of the picture is another aspect of immaturity, expected at the five or six year level. Since only the first picture needs to be moved on the initial item, a perseveration of former solutions may be maintained. Perseveration or inability to shift frame of reference is a classic sign of perceptual problems. On the other hand, a random interchange or shuffling may indicate that anxiety is interfering with problem solving.

Aside from arrangement of the cards per se, the child's verbal version of the story told by the cards is informative and should always be recorded. For example, he may be able to describe the major theme, but unable to fit the details together. Infantile themes can be directly informative; bizarre themes can clarify the extent of pathology. The "Thematic Apperception Test" aspects of the stories thus may give important clues to problem areas.

Picture Arrangement has a number of stories which readily elicit themes of "naughtiness" and subsequent punishment or escape (for example, fire setting, stealing, fishing). From these stimuli, punishment or morality themes may be triggered and dwelled upon to an extent that suggests the crucial importance of such ideas in the child's world.

Sometimes an incorrect story is told with the proper sequence, or a correct story given along with an incorrect sequence. In either case, faulty functioning is indicated. This may stem from disturbance of thought processes due to emotional reactions, or merely indicate a failure to check results, perhaps reflecting impulsiveness.

High scores should be examined for the presence of such factors as alertness to detail, forethought and planning ability, logical, sequential thought processes, and finally, interest in others and in social situations and social skills.

Low scores should be scrutinized to check such factors as problems in visual organization of reality as contrasted to lack of reality testing (for example, individual pictures placed horizontally (sideways) rather than vertically, or ordered from right to left, as compared to bizzare solutions not stemming from perceptual deficit). A low score can often result from a transient state of inattentiveness. Equally penalizing is an impulsive or anxiety-ridden orientation to action, with no delay mechanisms taking effect, and a failure to check minimal clues.

BLOCK DESIGN

Description and History

Block Design on the WISC consists of ten two-dimensional designs to be reproduced with multicolored blocks within time limits. Only red and white sides of the blocks are utilized, with the blue and yellow sides serving as distractors.

The first two designs are to be copied from the examiner's block construction rather than a picture, and given only to children below the age of 8 or to older suspected mental defectives.

Copying two-dimensional designs with colored blocks was first utilized by Kohs (1923) as a non-verbal way of measuring intelligence. The test was later adapted for use in the Grace Arthur Performance Scale (Form I) (Arthur, 1930).

Rationale

The ability to analyze, synthesize, and reproduce an abstract two-dimensional geometrical pattern is considered a valid criterion of intelligence.

What the Test Measures

Perception, analysis, synthesis, and reproduction of abstract designs are among the aspects measured by this subtest. Logic and reasoning must be applied to space relationships.

Non-verbal concept formation involving an implicit verbal manipulation is necessary. Visual-motor coordination is also measured.

Item Composition and Difficulty

The first two designs (A and B) of the 10 design set are given only to children below eight and to older suspected mentally retarded children. Designs A and B are copied by the child looking directly at the examiner's model, the first of which (A) he has reproduced in front of the child. The remaining eight designs are reproduced from a pictorial pattern shown to the child. The first seven patterns use four blocks, the last three call for nine blocks.

8. BLOCK DESIGN							

Design		Time	Pass-Fail	Score				
A. 45"		1		2				
		2		0 1				
B. 45"		1		2				
		2		0 1				
C. 45"		1		2				
		2		0 1				
1. 75"				0	21-75 4	16-20 5	11-15 6	1-10 7
2. 75"				0	21-75 4	16-20 5	11-15 6	1-10 7
3. 75"				0	26-75 4	21-25 5	16-20 6	1-15 7
4. 75"				0	21-75 4	16-20 5	11-15 6	1-10 7
5. 150"				0	66-150 4	46-65 5	36-45 6	1-35 7
6. 150"				0	81-150 4	66-80 5	56-65 6	1-55 7
7. 150"				0	91-150 4	66-90 5	56-65 6	1-55 7

CHART VIII. BLOCK DESIGN SUBTEST

Guilford factors for all items

Figural relations
Figural redefining
Figural selection

Item placement of average scores for three age levels

Age 7½ (average raw score 6) success through item C
Age 10½ (average raw score 16-20) success through item 2 or 3
Age 13½ (average raw score 29-33) success through 5 or 6

All designs are symmetrical and thus involve some degree of pattern repetition, either top-bottom or right-left.

In contrast to some of the other subtests, Block Design produces a good range of scores without the telescoping seen in such tasks as Digit Span. As mentioned previously, one of the problems of the WISC has been the lack of range in the tasks utilized.

At age 7½ the average child achieves a raw score of 6. This entails copying designs A, B, and C correctly from the examiner's model. Age 10½ brings a raw score of 16 to 20, which usually means success through design #3, depending on speed time bonuses (relatively rare at this age). At age 13½ a raw score of 29 to 33 is average. This usually includes design #5 plus varying time bonuses (Chart VIII).

Item difficulty as reported by Sutherland (1960) for average referred children age 7 to 15 was consistent with placement, although design #4 (the diagonal red square) was somewhat easier than #2 or #3, perhaps due to cumulative practice effects.

Carlton and Stacy (1955) reported the first three designs (A, B, C) to be extremely easy for their sample of mentally retarded children with a MA of 8 (88 per cent or better passed). There was a sudden drop on design #1, and little success from that point on, although design #4 was slightly easier than either #2 or #3.

Significant Differences between Block Design and Other Subtests

Hopkins and Michael (1961), reported that significant differences (.05) between subtests required at least 4 weighted score points when Block Design is paired with Information, Comprehension, Arithmetic, Similarities, and Picture Arrangement. This difference had to rise to 5 points or more when the other subtest was Digits, Picture Completion, Object Assembly, or Coding. However, a difference of only 3 points is significant when Block Design is paired with Vocabulary.

Factorial Age Variables

Block Design proved to be an excellent measure of general intelligence (G). It was also found to measure a factor known as Perceptual Organization, "the organization of visually perceived materials in the context of time limitations." Block Design, therefore, is one subtest which can be interpreted separately, as a specific measure of perceptual organization and spatial visualization ability, a quality shared with Object Assembly. This is beside its considerable contribution to the total test. Block Design can be considered. to be an excellent non-verbal measure of intelligence (Cohen, 1959).

Utilizing the Guilford Structure-of-Intellect components, all Block Design items are classified under three factors. The first is Figural Relations: To be aware of relations between observed forms or other figural (sensed) elements. The second is Figural Redefining: To effect a change of interpretation of a figural complex so that a prescribed figural unit is apparent. The third is Figural Selection: To judge rapidly which figural entities meet a stated criterion (Chart VIII).

Since this is the one subtest that Cohen found to reveal a specific factor of perceptual organization, it is of interest to see that only the last of the Guilford factors is attributed to any other subtest (Object Assembly), while the other two are limited to the present subtest alone.

Advantages

A relatively small degree of variation can be meaningful on this subtest. Further, Block Design performance may indicate perceptual problems (as noted above, it is factorially specific). It is an excellent non-verbal task involving reasoning, and has the virtue of not compressing the scores because of its adequate upper range or high ceiling. Chance variations in scores are particularly low. Finally, it is undoubtedly the most culture-fair of the subtests.

Limitations

Block Design has a rather high "floor" and the initial designs are particularly difficult for those of low mental age or low grade intelligence. Inclusion of easier designs would have been helpful.

Block design is susceptible to a learning set. Sudden insight into the process of analysis and synthesis sometimes occurs during early items of the test, with improved performance resulting thereafter.

Too high a premium may be placed on finger dexterity because of the time limits on this task. Block Design is somewhat slow to administer, because of the $2\frac{1}{2}$ minute time limit which must be given the child on later designs.

Summary of Interpretations

A number of screening implications may be found in Block Design performance. With subjects who for a variety of reasons may be unable to express themselves adequately in verbal terms, Block Design can provide a good non-verbal measure of reasoning. Convergent rather than divergent skills are called for; creativity is not particularly rewarded here. Detection of perceptual distortions can suggest further examination for "organic" problems.

One interesting screening implication concerns the child who places some of the blocks correctly and then fumbles or waits helplessly. It has been suggested that he comes from a home where the parents never let a child finish an assigned task, but rather did it themselves.[*]

This test permits observation of important work habits, reflected in the manner of approach to the block designs. Success is achieved by organizing moves in advance and then swiftly executing the pattern. How does the child proceed? A trial and error method may be successful (if it leads to insight as the pattern is produced). Fumbling with the blocks after completing most of the design suggests that the child has missed the principle that one part of the design is equivalent to another. A planless shuffling which yields no design indicates a tendency toward confusion. The child may change from one approach to another, for example, from analysis and synthesis to trial and error, as designs increase in complexity. The point at which this change occurs indicates how susceptible the youngster is to pressure and its effect on his performance. The extent of finger dexterity is readily observed on this test. Limitations here may indicate specific motor difficulties. Also, there may be a gap in the child's awareness that each design must be square. This sort of construction suggests that the basic ability to form simple concepts is faulty. Inability to grasp the concept involved in making a diagonal pattern (that is, by using the two-colored sides of the blocks) usually indicates a lag in perceptual development, since this should be achieved by seven years of age.

Constant spinning and turning of the blocks and, particularly, double twisting, when one block is rotated in each hand, is often evidence of overt anxiety expressed in excessive activity (due to impairment of inhibitory control). A different way of expressing anxiety occurs when a pattern is completed quickly and correctly with the exception of one block and the error is not spontaneously corrected; the hasty, inaccurate completion of the pattern is essentially unreflective. Perhaps this is evidence of the crippling effects of repression on the subject's awareness of the integrity of the pattern. The implication of this is an anxiety-avoidant flight from the problem.

Attempting to copy the sides of the pattern as well as the top on

---

[*] Saurenman, Rene: Personal communication, 1964.

designs A and B can indicate an unusually concrete approach to material or a compulsive, perfectionistic orientation: "You told me to copy it so I'm copying it every way I know how." This may also be used to show hostility to the examiner by an expression of over compliance. The ready triggering of hostility in such circumstances, on this or other subtests, should be noted as possibly indicating the child's typical response to demands of authority. Another hypothesis is that this construction represents an overalertness to details in the environment. Such overalertness is at times motivated by a general tendency to fear being accused of not doing exactly what one is told.

When blue-yellow rather than red-white patterns are used after the initial design, red-green color blindness should be suspected. If this is ruled out, the use of blue-yellow patterns is virtually always indicative of great immaturity and, thus in the older child, severe pathology, usually, but not exclusively, organic in nature. Younger children may resort to the blue-yellow pattern at the beginning of the series for reasons readily verbalized: "I just put four blocks together." However, in the ten year old, even initial satisfaction with such a solution suggests a low level of aspiration and questionable reality testing.

Summarizing, high scores should be examined for the presence of such factors as: good conceptualizing ability; analytic and synthesizing talents; speed and accuracy in sizing up a problem; rapid adoption of trial and error methods; flexibility rather than rigidity in problem solving; and excellent finger-eye coordination. Overemphasis of detail, matching block by block rather than grasping an over-all principle or concept is also helpful for a different but successful approach. Previous exposure to Kohs Blocks can explain sudden success.

Low scores can indicate such factors as perceptual problems and poor spatial conceptualization. Other possibilities include visual motor defects, insecurity and compulsive trends (note excessively slow and methodical approach), and possible color blindness. There may be excessive concern over unessential details such as minor color differentiations. These may indicate a compulsive need for accuracy, or a hostile rejection of the task through a negative use of perfectionism. Sometimes in the case of seriously disturbed reality testing, a child attempts bizarre solutions, for example, vertical construction. A very anxious child may manifest his disturbance in planless fumbling, failure to check pattern, and other random approaches. Lack of reflectiveness is shown in overly speedy, careless construction. Finally, a failure orientation is shown by a refusal to try for a solution (some-times seen in younger children, due to the high floor of the subtest).

OBJECT ASSEMBLY

Description and History

This test consists of four cut-up (jigsaw) picture puzzles of a man, a horse, a face, and an auto to be assembled within time limits. Time credits are given for speed.

The items were adapted from those devised by Pintner and first used in the Pintner-Paterson Scale (1921). Object Assembly was selected by Wechsler because it offered the advantage of a formboard type of test, yet has the necessary higher ceiling.

Rationale

The synthesis of parts into an organized, integrated whole is con-sidered to be one criterion of intelligence. The combining of parts is similar in a way to the task in Block Design, except that here the configurations are familiar objects rather than abstract geometrical de-signs, and final configuration must be deduced rather than copied.

What the Test Measures

This test calls for adequate perception, visual-motor coordination, and simple assembly skills. For success there must be some visual anticipation of part-whole relationships, and flexibility in working toward a goal which may be unknown at first. A synthesis of con-crete visual forms is required.

Object Assembly measures ability to assemble material drawn from life into a meaningful whole. It calls for the ability to see spatial relationships, as does Block Design, with one important difference: where the blocks must be assembled to match a pattern; the objects must be assembled with no clues beyond naming the "Boy" and the "Horse," and no leads at all for the "Face" and the "Car." Thus the child must look for the key to each object, figuring out in advance what he is constructing.

Item Composition and Difficulty

Object Assembly is made up of four disassembled objects, two of which are named for the child. The remaining two are presented without comment.

9. OBJECT ASSEMBLY												
Object	Time	Score										
M anikin 120"		0	1	2	3	21-120 4	16-20 5	11-15 6	1-10 7			
H orse 180"		0	1	2	3	4	5	31-180 6	21-30 7	16-20 8	1-15 9	
F ace 180"		0	1	2	3	4	5	71-180 6	46-70 7	36-45 8	1-35 9	
A uto 180"		0	1	2	3	4	5	46-180 6	31-45 7	26-30 8	1-25 9	

Copyright 1949, The Psychological Corporation, New York, New York

CHART IX. OBJECT ASSEMBLY SUBTEST

Guilford factors for all items

Spatial orientation
Visualization
Figural selection

Item placement of average scores for three age levels

Age 7½ (average raw score 14-15) some success on three of the four objects
Age 10½ (average raw score 21-22) some success on all objects
Age 13½ (average raw score 24) full success on all objects

At age 7½ a raw score of 14 to 15 is an average and some success is expected on 3 of the 4 designs. At the age of 10½ raw scores average 21 to 22 and partial success on three or four patterns is expected. From 10½ to 13½ there is little spread, the slight difference in favor of 13½ year olds reflecting a few more time bonuses. For the older group a raw score of 24 is average, with some success on all four items being typical (Chart IX).

In terms of item difficulty it is quite clear as corroborated by Sutherland (1960) that the Face item is more difficult than the Auto item. However, since all designs are given, placement is not of significance. Carlton and Stacy (1955) found that 90 per cent of mental retardates (MA 8) could achieve some level of success on all items.

Significant Differences between Object Assembly and Other Subtests

Hopkins and Michael (1961) note that large differences between Object Assembly and the other subtests are needed to reach the .05

level of significance. At least five points are necessary when Object Assembly is paired with eight of the subtests, with this rising to 6 points or more for Digits and Coding.

Factorial Age Variables

Object Assembly is a consistently poor measure of general intelligence (G) at all three age levels. The variation of scores is much more apt to be due to chance than to the admittedly low reliability of the items themselves. However, this subtest does appear to be measuring perceptual organization ability, or "non-verbal interpretation and/or organization of visual perceived materials against a time limit." Especially when paired with Block Design, it is a useful measure of this factor. Object Assembly is too unreliable to be used alone in interpretation without careful reservations (Cohen, 1959).

When analyzed in terms of the Structure-of-Intellect components, Object Assembly designs are classified under three factors. The first is Spatial Orientation: To be aware of consistent interrelations among forms or other figural elements, to be aware of invariant systemic properties. The second is Visualization: To comprehend the new figural interrelations of elements which result from an indicated change. The last, seen also in the previous subtest, is Figural Selection: To judge rapidly which figural entities meet a stated criterion (Chart IX).

Since Cohen interpreted this subtest as contributing to a factor of Perceptual Organization, in common with Block Design, it would appear to be Figural Selection which represents a perceptual organization component overlapping the two subtests.

Advantages

Object Assembly is a simple, intrinsically interesting test which appeals to the child as a welcome break from some of the other tasks. The face validity of the material is excellent. Other than Block Design, it is the only test combining perception and visual motor skill.

Limitations

This test is notably unreliable and erratic successes or failures may affect the IQ scores markedly. There is not an even progression of design difficulty, nor is there a satisfactory upper range for superior children. Practice effects on this subtest preclude satisfactory use in retesting. It is a slow test to set up and administer, and the car item is considerably easier than the face, which precedes it, and may frustrate the younger child unduly.

Summary of Interpretations

The ability to go from a number of parts to an integrated whole mentally, in advance of the actual manipulations, is an important conceptual task found in Object Assembly and not in Block Design. The blocks represent a more abstract and presumably "culture-fair" task; the objects involve more emotional loading due to the prior meanings and associations (for example, mutilated figure) which may be triggered. However, there are fewer such threats to the individual who is "down to earth" and relies on reality for his clues. In other words, Object Assembly is not difficult for children who are oriented toward concrete thinking, or action oriented. It thus helps to screen such children from the mentally retarded.

High scores may indicate motor skills, the freedom to explore new solutions, and use trial and error successfully. Relative success can also suggest low socio-economic background; because of the lack of verbal culture loading, it is often the highest subtest for this group (This is by no means general, however, as a study of low socio-economic children's records will indicate.) Low scores should be explored for the presence of minimal experience with construction tasks and/or lack of planning ability. Object Assembly may be relatively low in highly verbal children. Here the lack of interest in assembly tasks can be a factor; also the relatively low ceiling is penalizing. Very low scores suggest perceptual and/or visual-motor deficiencies.

An extremely high score (for example, 3 or more weighted points above the subject's average) often indicates a driving anxiety or agitation, or a compensatory emphasis on environmental manipulation as a way to handle the anxiety. Anxiety can also result in low scores; instead of speeding up manipulation of material and thereby achieving success, a child may become aimless to offset feelings of helplessness. At some point the interpersonal reaction, that is, with the examiner who is watching his behavior, may lead to a hopeless feeling and a completely disrupted performance. This in turn can reflect the child's response to pressure—for example, a good score on the easy items (perhaps when they are named and thus defined for him), followed by a collapse when the material becomes more complicated.

The Manikin is seldom missed or distorted. If this happens, severe disturbance is virtually certain. Reversing the legs indicates rigidity as well as perceptual difficulties, particularly if not corrected despite questioning. The same point applies to reversing the legs of the Horse, although the relatively slight perceptual distortion involved makes this less significant particularly for children younger than eight years of age. Two common errors on the Horse which do not appear to be pathognomonic in the younger child are leaving out the center section and placing it between the front chest section and the head to make a neck. Again, it is the relatively slight degree of distortion which minimizes the significance of this error.

The Auto represents adjustment to the everyday world, and is seldom a problem for a child by age 10. Reversing the door section is a measure of inattention to detail, and thus possibly a sign of anxiety, or impulsive carelessness. (However, the black line on the door is often mistaken for a hinge by younger children.)

CODING

Description and History

This test, which consists of a simple and an advanced form, requires the child to match and copy symbols in blank spaces provided on the test sheet, using a guide of symbols associated with simple shapes (Coding A) or numerals (Coding B). Time credit is given for speed. Coding A is for children under 8, with 43 symbols to be filled in; Coding B, for children over 8, with 93 symbols to be entered.

Rationale

This test is based on the concept that the ability to learn combinations of symbols and shapes or symbols and numbers and then to re-create these combinations with paper and pencil within a time limit is one criterion of intelligence.

What the Test Measures

When used with children this test seems to be measuring visual-motor dexterity, particularly pencil manipulation, more than anything else. Ability to absorb new material presented in an associative context is also called for. Speed and accuracy in making associations determines success.

Item Composition and Difficulty

At age 7½ children average 35 to 37 correct for the Coding A task, which involves all but the last row. At age 10½, 36 to 37 is the aver-

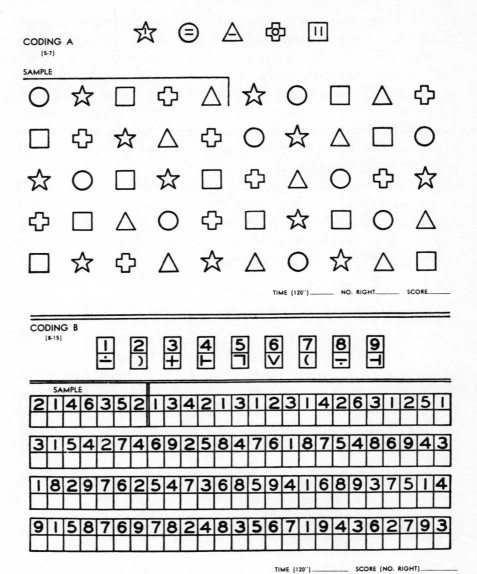

CHART X. CODING A OR B SUBTEST

Guilford factors for all items

Symbolic possibilities
Symbolic facility

Item placement of average scores for three age levels

Age 7½ (average raw score 35-37) items 35-37 Coding A, or end of fourth row
Age 10½ (average raw score 36-37) items 36-37 Coding B, or end of second row
Age 13½ (average raw score 45-48) items 45-48 Coding B, or beginning of third row

age age expected result for reproduction of Coding B, or toward the end of the second row. A raw score of 45 to 48 is average for 13½ year olds; this includes the beginning of the third row (Chart X). Item difficulty and placement are not problems on Digit Symbol, since there is no increase in difficulty.

Significant Differences between Coding and Other Subtests

Hopkins and Michael (1961) reported that for a significant difference (at the .05 level) between Coding and other subtests, the weighted subtest score variation had to be 5 points or more when Coding was paired with Information, Comprehension, Arithmetic, Similarities, Vocabulary, or Block Design, and at least 6 points when Coding was paired with Digits, Picture Completion, Picture Arrangement, or Object Assembly.

Factorial Age Variables

Coding scores make relatively little contribution to the measurement of general intelligence (G). Also, Coding does not contribute much to the factors which have been identified on the WISC. Random variation of scores is large. A specific factor of unknown significance is responsible for the bulk of Coding's reliable variance. This factor has not been associated with any known trait or ability. Taken alone, Cohen (1959) notes, Coding scores are of limited utility.

In terms of Structure-of-Intellect components, both Coding A and Coding B are classified under two factors: First, Symbolic Possibilities: To be aware of possible actions in a field of signs, numbers, or code elements, to eliminate redundancy is one kind of such action; and second, Symbol Facility (now including numerical facility): To recall rapidly expected results of stated actions on signs, numbers, and code elements (Chart X).

Cohen found Coding to load on its own, as yet undefined, factor. Perhaps the above represent a description of what this factor might represent.

Advantages

Coding is a rapid measure of the ability to learn a highly specific type of new task, and is one of the most rapidly administered subtests.

Limitations

Coding is often viewed by the child as a dull and uninspiring task; children are likely to become bored with it. Coding places a premium on compulsive drive rather than orientation to and competence in new learning. It thus seems to be measuring motivation rather than any aspect of intelligence.

People with low visual-motor coordination are inordinately penalized by Coding. Further, it has a limited spread of scores; very superior subjects often achieve little better than average scores on the subtest due to a combination of the factors noted above. Face validity is poor and the assumption that Coding tests the ability to learn different sorts of new material is highly dubious because of the specificity of the task and the many other factors mentioned above. In general Coding must be considered one of the poorest of the WISC subtests.

Summary of Interpretations

This subtest calls for rapid learning and copying or substituting new symbols. Since considerable effort is involved, the child is presented with problems in the area of acceptance and internalization of social standards (that is, a speedy performance upon command). In this sense Coding can be considered a measure of social adaptation, and hence maturity. A high degree of concentrated and sustained energy is necessary for a superior performance, something young children do not often possess. It is in this sense a test of mental as well as social adaptation. In general, bright, quick children do relatively poorly on this task, which requires a methodical, effortful, and even painstaking approach and does not permit variation of any kind. Typically, Coding is the lowest subtest in the profile of referred cases, so specific significance attributed to low scores must be considered carefully. However, some important behavioral signs may be observed on Coding. Difficulties in the receptive or expressive spheres (seeing versus copying) can indicate perceptual-motor problems at either the organic or functional levels.

High scores can be thought to result from a combination of high motivation (or compulsiveness), dexterity, and ability to memorize the symbols.

Low scores are frequently attributable to the absence of challenge in this task for many children. Other factors include specific visual defects, visual-motor coordination problems, and poor pencil control Associative inflexibility may lead to distortion of symbols (#5 reproduced as L instead of ⊥). Emotional distractability may lead to slapdash methods and failure to attend or concentrate. An action-oriented youngster may be too impulsive to achieve accuracy.

Loss of task orientation, revealed in the simplification of symbols to less complex shapes, or reproduction of symbols in sequential order without regard for the associated number printed above, suggests severe disturbance, perhaps reflecting organic factors, especially when reality contact (good task orientation) is established as adequate on the verbal tasks.

Skipping squares is rare except in the very young child. Occurring once or twice in the context of a good performance, it can indicate anxiety and a drive for achievement at the cost of accuracy. Occurring more often, it suggests severe distortion of reality at the perceptual level. Another indication of profound disturbance is the drawing of symbols which have no correspondence with the stimulus, or in other words, loss of contact with the presented task.

In this subtest it is possible for the child to work in ways which lead to success and yet not strictly follow instructions. For instance, a child can do a particular figure as it occurs, skipping all intervening ones. The tacit refusal to follow instructions ("Do not skip any") is important in its suggestion that the child is something of a rebel. In a good performance it also indicates the extent to which the child feels it necessary to win success through any means, proper or not.

Some children are so concerned about reproducing the designs exactly that they greatly slow down their performance. This perfectionistic trend is important to note, suggesting excessive striving to avoid failure in meeting external standards.

SUPPLEMENTARY TEST—VERBAL SCALE
DIGIT SPAN SUBTEST

Description and History

This subtest consists of two parts calling for a repetition of "digits forward" (ranging from a series of three through a series of nine) and "digits backward" (ranging from a series of two through a series of eight).

Probably memory span for digits has been used more than any other test in scales of intelligence. It forms part of the original Binet-Simon scale as well as all subsequent revisions of this original intelligence measure. It has been used widely and for a long time by psychiatrists as a test of simple retentiveness. However, as a test of general intelligence it ranks among the poorest. Memory span for either digits forward or backwards correlates very poorly with all other tests of intelligence.

This kind of item was included on the WISC by Wechsler, however, primarily for two reasons other than measurement of general intelligence. First, it is a good measure at the lower age levels. Except in cases of organic defect or other special circumstances, children by 7½ years of age who cannot remember four digits forward and two backwards probably will have some degree of mental deficiency. Second, difficulty with repetition of digits forwards or backwards is often of diagnostic significance with respect to attention span and concentration. As a result, then, of this test's good discrimination at the lower limits of intelligence and because it serves as an excellent diagnostic tool, Wechsler included it in all Wechsler scales.

Rationale

The underlying assumptions of this subtest are threefold. It makes the assumption that rote memory is one of those abilities of which a certain absolute minimum is required for all levels of intellectual functioning. However, excesses above this absolute minimum seemingly contribute relatively little to the capacity of the child to function as a whole. It appears then to be one of those abilities which enter into intellectual functioning only as necessary minima. Another assumption which this test makes is its importance as a good measure of intellectual functioning at the lower ability levels. This test also has the underlying assumption that repetition of digits forwards and backwards may be of diagnostic significance. A marked falling off of rote memory span is often one of the earliest indications of many types of disorganization, organic as well as functional. It may demonstrate poor ego control, anxiety, and inability to suspend irrelevant thought processes while attending to a task. Unlike the other verbal tests, however, Digit Span does not make the assumption that children of greater ability, higher curiosity, and broader interests will have greater success in repeating digits forwards and backwards. Possibly the higher ability child will grasp more quickly how to group the numbers which insures higher success on this test, but this is not always true.

What the Test Measures

This part of the scale is an attempt to determine the level of a child's ability to attend in a rather simple situation. It is an attempt to measure immediate auditory recall or immediate auditory memory (attention) span. If the child understands and masters methods of grouping operations, his success on this test probably is assured. In this sense then attention becomes an active as well as a passive process. Also of crucial importance for success on this test is the child's level of mental alertness. If he can suspend irrelevant thought processes while attending to this task his capacity for success on digits will be high. It might be noted, however, that a score on this test considerably above the subtest average can and often does indicate flattened affect or bland emotional life and a classical repression of feeling.

Difficulty with digits in most cases indicates impaired attention. Besides the possibility of brain damage, long recognized as affecting the memory process and immediate recall, this test also reflects the effects of anxiety and the inability for self-control of mental operations. The ability to repeat more digits backward than forward may indicate a sudden "catching on" to the task. It may also indicate stubbornness; the child rejects the "too easy" task of repeating digits forward, but feels challenged by the need to reverse the digits. Conceivably this might be a child who is highly motivated to intellectual tasks but only of his own choosing. The ability to do better on reversed than forward digits thus is often due to the child's independence and intellectual strivings which probably only emphasize difficult tasks. A reversed score then which equals or exceeds a digit forward score may be an indication of various factors: mental control and flexibility, good stress tolerance, possibly bland emotional tone, even negativism, i.e., rejecting the simple test of digits forward, and/or the interest in rising to a challenge.

Gross discrepancy between digits forwards and digits backward in favor of digits forward suggests excessive rigidity in thinking or, more seriously, a tendency for thinking to fragmentize under pressure. It may represent an evidence of effortful striving. This also occurs in cases of concrete thinking with corresponding inability to shift the frame of reference or even comprehend the task of reversing. Decided fluctuation of functioning on this test can also be an indication of lapses in attention due to either heightened anxiety, which may cause withdrawal from the situation, or in some cases to an inability to control mental processes so that the child continuously talks and makes little further effort to attend to the threatening situation.

High scores on this test can indicate several things. The child may have a good rote memory and good immediate recall. He may be able to remain calm and thus attend well in a testing situation. Low

DIGIT SPAN			
Digits Forward	Score (Circle)	Digits Backward	Score (Circle)
3-8-6 6-1-2	3 3	2-5 6-3	2 2
3-4-1-7 6-1-5-8	4 4	5-7-4 2-5-9	3 3
8-4-2-3-9 5-2-1-8-6	5 5	7-2-9-6 8-4-9-3	4 4
3-8-9-1-7-4 7-9-6-4-8-3	6 6	4-1-3-5-7 9-7-8-5-2	5 5
5-1-7-4-2-3-8 9-8-5-2-1-6-3	7 7	1-6-5-2-9-8 3-6-7-1-9-4	6 6
1-6-4-5-9-7-6-3 2-9-7-6-3-1-5-4	8 8	8-5-9-2-3-4-2 4-5-7-9-2-8-1	7 7
5-3-8-7-1-2-4-6-9 4-2-6-9-1-7-8-3-5	9 9	6-9-1-6-3-2-5-8 3-1-7-9-5-4-8-2	8 8

F_____ + B_____ = _____
Highest numbers circled

CHART XI. SUPPLEMENTARY TEST—VERBAL SCALE
DIGIT SPAN SUBTEST

Guilford factors

Digits Forward—Memory span
Digits Backward—Memory for symbol patterns

Item placement of average scores for three age levels

Age 7½ (average raw score 8) success on 4 or 5 digits forward, 3 or 4 digits backward
Age 10½ (average raw score 9) success on 5 digits forward, 4 digits backward
Age 13½ (average raw score 10) success on 5 or 6 digits forward, 4 or 5 digits backward

scores on this test may be indicative that there is a hearing deficit in the child, that he may be highly susceptible to fatigue, that he may be consciously anxious, and possibly that there may be organic concomitants which may have great affect upon attention. Depressive trends could be indicated by an isolated low subtest score here which may stem from an inability to rally to an immediate task.

Item Composition and Difficulty

This part of the test employs items in number form and includes items through 9 digits forward and eight digits backward. All items are presented orally with each digit in the item presented at the rate of one per second. Each item has one alternate set of numbers in the event that the first set is missed or is invalidated because of extraneous noise factors. As discussed above, the digits forward items are examples of the more passive auditory immediate recall type of item while digits backwards are examples of the more active auditory recall items. Obviously, the items on this test are not highly influenced by knowledge received in the public school setting. Bright children are probably unduly penalized on this test for they are not sufficiently challenged to show their talents; if they do have success, they find the ceiling much too low.

As is true of the other tests on the WISC, level of success with these items is dependent upon the age of the child. Unlike the other tests, however, scores achieved at various age levels change very little. At 7½ years of age a raw score of 8 is average, which is typically obtained by passing five digits forward (8-4-2-3-9) and three backward (5-7-4). By 10½ years of age however an increase of only one raw score point is expected so that an average score of 9 is obtained at this age. This is typically achieved by passing five forward (8-4-2-3-9) and four backwards (7-2-9-6). At the uper age level, i.e., 13½ years of age, only one more point is expected for the average child, making 10 the average raw score at this age. Typically this is achieved by passing five forward (8-4-2-3-9) and five backward (4-1-3-5-7) (Chart XI).

Placement of items in this subtest is obviously not a problem as in the other tests of this scale. Thus all items included in the subtest are placed according to increasing serial numbers starting with three digits forward and going through nine forward; and with digits backwards starting with two digits backwards and going to eight digits. Again, it should be noted that the child has two sets of digits at each serial level.

When Carlton and Stacey (1955), studying item placement, analyzed the results found with their mentally retarded sample with an average mental age of 8 years they found that 90 per cent of their sample passed four digits forward. However at this point there semed to be a dramatic increase in difficulty for these children. As for digits backward, 87 per cent of this sample could pass two digits backwards. However, from this point on again there was the same dramatic increase in difficulty as appeared after four digits forwards.

The unusually limited range of scores through ages 7½-13½ permits little discrimination in terms of either mental or chronological age. It therefore contributes very little to the understanding of the subject's intellectual functioning and operations except in cases of low ability levels, and some cases of organic and functional deficits. A good rote memory is of practical value but correlates very little with the higher levels of intellectual processes. For this reason, Wechsler (1958) combined digits forwards and digits backwards into only one test, reducing the amount which each contributes to the total score. Because of the low correlation with general intelligence it did not appear reasonable to give these two types of items as much weight as the other tests on the scale. Thus, by combining the two, they contribute only 1/12 of the total score, whereas if they were separated they would have contributed much more heavily.

Significant Differences between Digit Span and Other Subtests

Hopkins and Michael (1961) in their analysis of significant differences between Digit Span and other subtests found that when Digit Span is paired with one of the following, namely, Information, Comprehension, Arithmetic, Similarities, Vocabulary, Picture Arrangement or Block Design, there must be weighted score difference of at least 5 points to obtain a statistically significant difference at the 5 per cent level. For a significant difference to appear between Digit Span and Picture Completion, Object Assembly or Coding (Digit Symbol), a difference of 6 points is required.

Factorial Age Variables

When Cohen (1959) factor analyzed the standardized date of the WISC, he found that Digit Span by itself does not measure either general intelligence memory or freedom from distractability. Further, the reliability of this subtest was found to be the poorest of any of the WISC subtests.

At the older age level (13½) a factor hypothesized as reflecting "freedom from distractability" appears and contributes substantially. However, this measurement requires a combination of Digit Span and Arithmetic for interpretation.

It would appear then that Digit Span is a poor measure of intelligence and that specific interpretations as a measure of freedom from distractability should be made very hesitantly until the older age levels.

On the Guilford Structure-of-Intellect components, Digits Forward are classified under one factor: Memory Span: To reproduce immediately arbitrary groups of sign, digit, or letter series. Digits Backward are classified under a different factor: Memory for Symbol Patterns: To reproduce or recall interrelations among signs or code element (Chart XI). This is a case of clear disagreement with Cohen's analysis. Memory did not appear as a factor when the standardization data were utilized.

Advantages

The subtest serves as a rapid check on verbal memory and attention. The child's approach to this emotionally neutral situation gives clues to his efficiency in handling simple tasks. Failure suggests inability to concentrate and hence low frustration tolerance for tasks involving a minimum of difficulty.

The test is quickly administered and is non-threatening in that the child is not aware of glaring errors. All these factors build confidence in the overall task.

Limitations

The extremely limited range of scores makes this a very poor measure of intellectual growth or even of functioning at any particular level. More basically, there is definite question about the correlation of rote memory with general intelligence. Furthermore, it is unusually vulnerable to temporary disturbances of concentration and attention.

Summary of Interpretations

The areas of concentration and attention are particularly important in this subtest. The narrow range of average scores between the various age levels would seem to indicate little difference in this factor due to maturation. A wide discrepancy (more than two) between forward and reversed digits in favor of digits forward could represent an avoidance of effortful striving. This also occurs in cases of concrete thinking with corresponding inability to shift the frame of reference or even to comprehend the task of reversal. In contrast, the ability to do better on reversed rather than forward digits can be thought of as a clue to the child's independence of thought, lack of rigidity, and desire to excel since to succeed in this particular way is difficult. It also shows good tolerance for stress. Sometimes this pattern may reflect negativism—rejection of the more simple task of digits forward.

Low scores can indicate such problems as possible hearing loss, concomitants which may affect attention, or a depressive trend stemming from inability to rally to the immediate task. Very commonly, however, a low score is due to the presence of manifest anxiety.

SUPPLEMENTARY TEST—PERFORMANCE SCALE
MAZES

Description and History

This subtest consists of eight mazes, the first two given only to children under the age of eight or to older suspected mental defectives.

Porteus (1965) first used paper and pencil maze problems as a criterion for intelligent behavior in 1913. Their success was confirmed by their inclusion in the Army Beta or Performance scale, utilized in World War I (Yerkes, 1921).

Rationale

This subtest is based on the concept that the ability to plan ahead ("preherse" according to Porteus) and move accurately through a paper maze is a meaningful criterion of intelligence.

What the Test Measures

Mazes call first for planning and foresight, for attention to instructions such as the request not to lift the pencil, for pencil control and hence visual-motor coordination, and for speed combined with accuracy.

Item Composition and Difficulty

Eight mazes including two (A and B) given to younger children compose this test. At age $7\frac{1}{2}$ the average child receives a raw score of 10 to 11 or credit for Maze #3, depending on errors. At age $10\frac{1}{2}$ the average child receives a raw score of 16 or some credit for Maze #5 and at age $13\frac{1}{2}$ the average child receives a raw score of 17 or some credit on all the Mazes; between $10\frac{1}{2}$ and $13\frac{1}{2}$ there is little increase in range therefore and hence poor discrimination of ability in terms of age adequacy (Chart XII).

Maze difficulty is not reported by Sutherland (1960). Carlton and Stacy (1955) report that 70 per cent of their mentally retarded sample (MA 8) succeeded in doing Maze #2, and over 30 per cent succeeded to some extent on the last problem.

MAZES			
Maze	Max. Errors	Errors	Score
A. 30"	2		0 1 2
B. 30"	2		0 1 2
C. 30"	2		0 1 2
1. 30"	3		0 1 2 3
2. 45"	3		0 1 2 3
3. 60"	5		0 1 2 3
4. 120"	6		0 1 2 3
5. 120"	8		0 1 2 3

CHART XII. SUPPLEMENTARY TEST—PERFORMANCE SCALE
MAZES SUBTEST

Guilford factor for all items

Perceptual foresight

Item placement of average scores for all three age levels

Age 7½ (average raw score 10-11) success to maze 2 or 3
Age 10½ (average raw score 16) success to maze 5
Age 13½ (average raw score 17) success to maze 5

Statistical Significant Differences between Mazes and Other Subtests

No data are available on this subtest, which is not used frequently.

Factorial Age Variables

While Mazes do not contribute much to the measure of general intelligence (G), it is considered a useful subtest on the basis of Cohen's (1959) analysis. The error variance is much lower than that of most of the other performance subtests, enhancing what contribution it does make.

At ages 7½ and 10½, Mazes contributes substantially to the measurement of perceptual organization ("non-verbal interpretation and/or organization of visually perceived materials against a time limit"). Mazes are especially useful in measuring perceptual organization when combined with Block Design and Object Assembly. However, by age 13½ this is no longer true.

More than any other subtest, Mazes measures something specific, which can probably be labeled "planning ability" or "prehersal" (see Porteus).

On the Guilford Structure-of-Intellect components, Mazes are classified under one factor: Perceptual Foresight: To be aware of possibilities implicit in a figural context (Chart XII). The agreement with the
Cohen analysis is probably higher here than for any other subtest.
However, there is no reference to the overlap with other performance
tests noted by Cohen.

Advantages

Particularly with non-verbal children, Mazes is useful as an additional non-word oriented subtest. There is an element of play in the
task which appeals to many children. Foresight is emphasized.

Limitations

Mazes have a number of disadvantages. The subtest is not properly
standardized as part of the WISC. In addition, there is an insufficient
range of scores. Correlation with total score is poor, a point tying in
with the fact that this subtest is seldom administered and thus not a
regular part of the battery; hence its inclusion in the total score
may make the overall IQ not too comparable with the IQ derived
from the standard battery. The rule about not lifting the pencil calls
for considerable alertness on the part of the examiner to be sure the
child adheres to the instructions on which the test was standardized.

Summary of Interpretations

Perhaps the most valuable aspect of Mazes lies in the opportunity
to observe the child's planning in a new situation, which reflects itself in the score obtained. High scores reflect planning efficiency
which is highly correlated with an ability to delay impulsive action.
They also suggest adequate visual-motor coordination. Low scores
suggest the reverse: impulsivity and poor visual-motor coordination.
If considerably lower than the other subtests, orientation to reality
may be poor.

SUBTEST ANALYSIS BIBLIOGRAPHY

Anderson, Jane M.: Review of the WISC. In Buros, O. K., Ed., *The Fourth
    Mental Measurement Yearbook.* Highland Park, New York: Gryphon Press,
    1953, 477-479.
Arthur, Grace: *A Point Scale of Performance Tests.* New York: The Common-
    wealth Fund, 1930.
Bonsall, Marcella R. and Meeker, Mary M.: Structure of intellect components
    in the WISC. Los Angeles County Superintendent of Schools, Division of
    Research and Guidance, Programs for the Gifted, 1964.

Carleton, F. O. and Stacey, C. L.: An item analysis of the WISC. *J. clin. Psychol.* 1955, 11, 149-154.

Cohen, J.: The factorial structure of the WISC at ages 7½, 10½, and 13½. *J. consult. Psychol.* 1959, 23, 285-299.

Cornell, E. L. and Coxe, W. W.: *A Performance Ability Scale.* New York: Harcourt, Brace and World, 1934.

Delattre, Lois and Cole, D.: A comparison of the WISC and the Wechsler Bellevue. *J. consult. Psychol.* 1952, 16, 228-230.

Guilford, J. P. and Merrifield, P. R.: The structure-of-intellect model: its uses and implications. Report from the Psychological Laboratory #24, USC, 1960.

Hopkins, K. D. and Michael, W. B.: The diagnostic use of WISC subtest patterns. *Calif. J. educ. Res.* 1961, 12, 116-117, 130.

Kohs, S. C.: *Intelligence Measurement.* New York: The Macmillan Co., 1923.

Kuhlman, F. and Anderson, Rose G.: *Kuhlman-Anderson Intelligence Tests.* Princeton, New Jersey: Personnel Press, 1927.

Pintner, R. and Patterson, D.: *A Point Scale of Performance Tests.* New York: Appleton-Century Crofts, 1917.

Porteus, S. D.: *The Maze Test and Clinical Psychology.* Palo Alto, California: Pacific Books, 1965.

Rappaport, D. et al.: *Diagnostic Psychological Testing,* Vol. I and II. Chicago: Year Book Publishers, 1946.

Seashore, H. G. et al.: The standardization of the WISC. *J. consult. Psychol.* 1950, 14, 99-110.

Sullivan, Elizabeth T. et al.: *California Test of Mental Maturity.* Montery, California: California Test Bureau, 1957.

Sutherland, S. P.: A study of the difficulty gradient of the WISC subtest items. Unpublished paper, USC, 1960.

Wechsler, D.: *The Measurement of Adult Intelligence.* Baltimore: The Williams and Wilkins Co., 1944.

——: *The Measurement and Appraisal of Adult Intelligence.* Baltimore: The Williams and Wilkins Co., 1958.

——: *Wechsler Intelligence Scale for Children, Manual.* New York: The Psychological Corporation, 1949.

Yerkes, R. M.: *Psychological Examining in the United States Army.* Memoirs of the National Academy of Sciences, 1921, 15, Washington, D.C., Government Printing Office.

IV

GENERALIZED PROJECTIVE ASPECTS

The rich samples of behavior which can be obtained during the administration of the WISC are often far more important than any numerical scores on the subtests and verbal and performance scales. With relatively few items to administer on each subtest, the examiner must be well aware that the reliability of scores on the subtests can be very low. But when the interrelationship between the sub-test and the qualitative aspects of the child's approach to the test and actual responses are added, the reliability of findings may be greatly enhanced.

In this chapter, the facets of the test which may reveal crucial personality attributes, or what has been called the "style" of the performance are examined to reveal how a child functions and what may be expected from him.

The test of intelligence provides information on patterns of past intellectual achievement, current problem-solving methods, and the ability to verbalize meaningfully. Further, such a test reflects adaptive and defensive aspects of the personality, rigidity or flexibility of thinking, and the extent to which ordinarily impersonal, detached intellectual functions are invaded by emotional conflicts. It goes without saying that children are much more open to such invasion than are adults, and that a sure measure of increasing maturity is the ability to screen emotional intrusions from problem-solving situations which call for cognitive responses. However, the separation of these two aspects of functioning is a relative matter, for each child has a unique style of approach to life situations, made up of a composite of elements.

While important personality variables have been elicited from the analysis of the adult Wechsler scales (see Rapaport et al., 1945; Schafer, 1948; Shapiro, 1954; and others), specific applications of the projective approach to the WISC have been limited (Fromm et al., 1957; Fromm, 1960). In contrast, there has been more use of scatter or pattern analysis (using patterns of high and low scores characterizing the test profiles of children considered to fit into various diagnostic categories), which is an "actuarial" approach comparable to the predictions made from life insurance expectancy tables. The avoidance of a dynamic consideration of behavior, or in other words, the "why" of each response, and the emphasis on placing each subject in a given diagnostic category, such as "brain-damaged" or "behavorial problem," have led to insignificant results. This approach has not been successful because, among other reasons, a generally accepted nosology or classification of children's adjustment problems has not yet been developed. Even assuming such a nosology would be available, however, the simple classification of children into categories would still result in the overlooking of rich individual dynamics to be found in any one person, regardless of his problem category. Such classification would assume that simple categorizing tells us more of a child's learning ability and personality development than an analysis of his individuality.

In the following pages, aspects of the WISC which go beyond the plus and minus of given answers and involve "projective" aspects will be discussed. In other words, what the child "puts into" his answers, how he goes about approaching the test situation and the examiner, and why he selects one answer rather than another will be explored, and the rationale underlying the application of such aspects to specific test protocols will be spelled out.

A variety of hypotheses which might describe and explain certain test behaviors will be presented. None of the hypotheses is to be considered in any way as a sure or absolute definition of behavior described. Instead, they are presented in the hope that they may serve to stimulate the thinking of the examiner in his search for meaningful test behavior.

EXAMINER VARIABLES

Prior to analysis of the projective aspects of the child's behavior, we would first like to describe what we may call examiner variables. From the moment the examiner meets the child he is about to examine, he can observe a wide variety of reactions which relate to the child's attitude toward the examiner. To interpret such reactions with greatest accuracy, the examiner, as mentioned previously, should be aware of his own contribution to the test situation. Each individual must also learn his own characteristics as an examiner. For example, does he present himself as a teacher-asking-for-right-answers? A permissive grandparent? An admired expert? A laissez-faire parent? A threatening principal? Only after a long period of experience testing children with and without problems do most individuals discover the role they project when giving the WISC. Beginning examiners, unsure of themselves in their new role, may assume that the child is aware of their desire to treat him as an equal. Only after much experience do they realize that the child equates them with a-doctor-who-gives-shots who looks-for-something-wrong. For younger children, the sex of the examiner may prove crucial. Thus, female examiners can readily fall into the mother-teacher model, while male examiners may automatically be classified as a threatening father-principal. Cieutat (1965) has reported that female examiners elicited Binet IQ's significantly higher than those obtained by male examiners.

The issue to be resolved in terms of how the examiner is viewed by the child is not so much to carve out a neutral role of WISC giver, but instead to recognize how children tend to view him, and then use that knowledge to describe how the individual child reacts to that kind of person. A simple example is the rather motherly, easy-going woman examiner who is reacted to as an ogre by a particular child. From her experience, she knows that the average child finds her not at all threatening. The fact that this child reacts in a terrified manner may tell a great deal about the child. Another example is the basically matter-of-fact, practical, no-nonsense young male examiner who is aware that children are in awe of his test manner. When he examines a boy who sits on the edge of the desk, pops up and down with no attempts at self-control, whistles loudly as he works, and accuses the examiner of "tricking" him, he is able to conclude that this test behavior was not induced by the examiner's covert acceptance (as deduced by its rarity in his experience) and could be characteristic of a poorly controlled little boy who has not accepted authority.

CHILD VARIABLES

We now consider material relating to behavior of the child rather than the examiner. This behavior can be elicited by any of the subtests presented, or in the response to the examiner and to the implications of "being tested." In the following, some of the observable variables are examined.

These variables are presented in terms of antonyms, or extremes in order to encourage the examiner to look at test behavior not only as the "defensive" means of adjusting to the pressure of being examined and, by extension, to the pressure of "test-like" situations in everyday life, but also as the "adaptive" means of adjusting to such situations. In other words, a child's behavior is seen as existing on a continuum, to use a simplified model, from that which represents an ideal adjustment to life to that which represents a pathological adjustment to life. Often only delicate shadings of difference separate good from poor adjustment, as the following examples will reveal.

Although there is much overlap in many of the following terms, the slightly differing shades of meaning may result in different emphasis, and thus give broader insight than possible were the terms to be compressed.

Hesitant Response

RESERVE: A certain degree of reserve, especially in the initial period of contact with the examiner, is a normal sign in school-age children and, in fact, should be expected as an indication of good adjustment. Thus, initially, the child volunteers very little spontaneously, answers what he is asked and no more, and generally holds back until he is sure of the situation and what is expected of him.

In contrast, extreme shyness can be observed in the child's holding back from responding to the examiner, even after a period of getting acquainted. When this behavior continues to the point of limiting responses, problems are indicated. Is the examiner seen as a threatening adult? By analogy, does this suggest a tendency to see adults (parents, teachers) as frightening or demanding? In the classroom, such a child will need constant attention and urging to elicit a response. (Children with school phobia may show such a pattern.) In rare cases, extreme shyness represents a severe withdrawal, indicating the child is no longer in contact with those about him. In such cases, other behavioral signs of disturbance are prominent. When differentiating between normal reserve and excessive shyness, the examiner must be alert to the amount of time required to establish rapport, the degree of encouragement required to elicit a response, and the extent to which this pattern reverses with the passage of time.

APPREHENSION: A slightly different shading of the hesitant behavior might be characterized as on a continuum from responsive apprehension to manifest anxiety. The unknown test situation is, basically, not the most comforting experience to face. Therefore, any child who is aware of the fact that life is sometimes difficult can be expected to view the examiner as something of a threat. A certain degree of apprehension is thus a sign of adaptive ability. However, when this cannot be overcome even after the child has been introduced to the text experience, when open nervousness continues without abatement, the examiner may speculate that this is a child who finds it difficult to face any new situation. He will be alert to the extent that this nervous reaction is likely to affect test responses.

SELF-PROTECTION: Still another shading of the hesitant behavior might be characterized as ranging from self-protectiveness to defensiveness. At the adaptive end of the continuum one would expect a child to hesitate in making wild guesses or attempting items far beyond his chronological age level. At the other end of the continuum would be the child who finds even the initial questions too threatening, for example, the twelve year old who refused to say at what kind of a store we buy sugar, defensively maintaining that his mother did not take him shopping. In such a case, the examiner might speculate that the youngster views the examination as so threatening or as such a possible source of ridicule that he is unwilling to expose himself. These defensive reactions might take several forms. For example, statements such as, "It doesn't go together" or "They *aren't* the same!" may indicate a fear of becoming emotionally involved, of exploring one's own reactions. The remark, "I can't do it," on the other hand, may indicate passivity, resignation, and a feeling of being threatened by others.

Active Response

The previous examples stressed atmospheres of hesitancy in the examination. The following examples will cover more active approaches to the examiner.

FRIENDLINESS: One continuum here might be called relating versus overfriendliness. Ideally, the well adjusted child should view the examiner as a helpful and interested adult. Actually, few situations are as rewarding for a child as individual testing. In spite of the initial concern about the situation, most children find themselves for the first time in their lives on the receiving end of complete adult attention. Every word they utter is solemnly recorded, every answer they give is seriously considered by an attentive grownup. Therefore, it is not surprising that the average child quickly relates to this fascinating adult. By contrast, an extreme and maladaptive form of this relating might be called overfriendliness. Sometimes this compares to the puppy-like attachment characteristic of the preschool child, and thus represents immaturity. Other times, overfriendliness represents the child's rather touching need to ingratiate himself with an adult who might otherwise be dangerous.

INITIATIVE: Another form of relationship is the continuum running from initiative to brashness. The well-adjusted child can take certain initiative in the test situation. Thus, he begins the various items as they are presented, and let us know when he is done. At the other extreme is brashness, a form of behavior which was found to relate to poor judgment as evaluated by psychiatrists (Lambert and Zimmerman, 1964). In this, the child attempts to take over the examiner's role. Impertinent questioning ("You tell ME the answer!"), refusal to remain seated during the testing, answering back, and other such inappropriate reactions indicate an inability to restrain behavior, and a tendency to act out negative feelings. Such behavior in the test room may be assumed to characterize the child who in the school setting is unable to behave appropriately and tends to act out angry feelings. This sort of behavior in the classroom can lead to rejection of the child by others, which in turn serves as an impetus to further retaliatory acting out.

CONFIDENCE: A further shading of a more active approach to the examiner can be labeled as the continuum from confidence to a need to impress. A child who is confident is not afraid to show the examiner that he can accomplish something. This may be done in such a way as to indicate a healthy acceptance of the need to do well, both from the standpoint of the response to the test and the relationship to the examiner. Effortful striving is assumed, as well as the ability to risk failure or hazard a guess. At the other pole can be seen the need to impress. Thus, the child may stress his own ability, deride the difficulty of items, and insist on his own adequacy ("I'm right, I've got an encyclopedia!"). Excesses in this direction indicate insecurity, and can be used as a measure of the degree to which the child must rely on the denial of inadequacy to get along. Such denial may indicate extreme inability to tolerate the frustration of "not knowing," which is, after all, an essential ingredient of the educational process. The bluffing and facade of adequacy which result may be observed in the classroom as leading to a vicious circle of refusing to learn, falling farther behind, and eventually being unable to catch up. The need to impress can be an important yardstick of the child's reaction to his teacher and his adjustment in the classroom.

ENERGY: Another reaction during testing can be labeled energetic versus hyperactive behavior. Ideally, the child being tested shows some degree of animation. He approaches test material with verve, works rapidly amassing time bonuses, and can keep up a steady flow of energy for the hour required to complete the WISC. Hyperactivity, in contrast, is seen in the child unable to sit still. He twists the booklet, piles up the blocks rather than waiting for the next pattern to be presented, tips his chair back until he is in immediate danger of landing on the floor. He wiggles, leaves the table, grabs at anything within reach. Such behavior has long been associated with children who have some degree of brain damage, although it is by no means a constant and reliable sign. Because hyperactivity is associated with a low attention span as well as overt anxiety, it typically indicates immaturity (where a limited attention span is characteristic).

SPEED: Somewhat related to the above is a continuum of behavior from speedy to impulsive. The WISC has many timed subtests, so some degree of speed is obviously rewarded on this test. Ideally, the child works rapidly, quickly sizing up the problem and starting to work. A particular style of some children is to use a speedy alternation of responses (trial and error) where another child might sit and think out his moves. At times the trial and error approach proves to be a marked advantage, as when, for example, in Block Design #6, the child discovers the method needed to create diagonal stripes by putting two diagonal colored blocks together. Often an accidental juxtaposition of blocks leads the child to the insight needed to solve certain patterns. At the other extreme, speed may descend into impulsivity: manipulating objects with no prior consideration of their meaning or no observation of the results; blurting out responses without due consideration. This is characteristic of the very young child; in children eight years and older it suggests immaturity or regression. Impulsivity may also indicate a deliberate avoidance of preliminary reflection, perhaps because such delay would allow the child to become aware of feelings which are highly anxiety-arousing. The impulsivity may also reveal emotional attitudes which should ideally be suppressed: for example, on Comprehension item #4 (when someone much smaller tries to start a fight), "Beat up on 'em!" or "Run home to Mommy!" are inappropriate responses for school-age children.

Obedience

The testing situation is basically an authoritarian setting, in which the examiner assigns tasks for the child to complete. Therefore, a degree of obedience is ideal in this setting. The child should sit where he is told, do each task he is assigned, and generally follow directions. Such meeting of adult standards is actually basic to doing well on the WISC. On the other hand, there can be an extreme form of this behavior which veers into dependency. Here the child presents each response hesitantly or interrogatively, waiting for approval before daring to continue. He seems afraid of disobeying the examiner; constant reassurance is required. Performance material is not approached spontaneously once presented; the examiner is beseeched to say again what to do or when to start. This role frequently reflects simple immaturity or retardation, but may also indicate emotional problems as well. Anxiety, for example, is apt to leave a person unable to trust his own judgment and thus dependent on others for clues how to perform. Repeated use of the passive tense, such as "that's what my teacher said," or of interrogative forms, "Isn't it?" suggests the passive receptive avoidance of responsibility. This lack of initiative, continuing throughout the examination, suggests passivity, immaturity, and possible anxiety relating to authority figures, as when the child dares do nothing in order to avoid doing something wrong. Dependency can be an important factor to consider in selecting the best teacher for a specific child.

SEARCH FOR CLUES: A fine shading of the above continuum of obedience to dependency is guided clue-seeking as compared to over-questioning. A child who is not extremely impulsive is likely to look to the adult for clues as to what is expected of him. Ideally, parents serve as prompters for school-age children, with sotto voce reminders to "say thank you" or "shake hands." From such a background, it is not surprising that certain children will continuously check with the examiner, usually by a quick glance, to see that they are on the right track. However, this can reach an extreme of presenting all responses in a questioning manner, adding a constant, "Did I do right?", or destroying accurate constructions because the examiner's expectant waiting for the child to announce that he is through is interpreted as criticism. Especially when the child must ask whether the simplest verbal answers are right (for example, Information #4: What animal gives us milk? "Cow, right? Is it right? Is it?"), there is an implication of "fading" of what should be overlearned material in the presence of considerable anxiety. Perplexity and impotence, classic signs of severe brain damage in adults (Piotrowski, 1957), can also be observed to underlie the questioning tone. If anxiety is the crucial variable, there may be marked improvement when support and approval are forthcoming. The point at which questioning is most prominent (at the initiation of testing, at the upper levels, or when "traumatic" material is presented) can be observed to have important classroom corollaries. For example, the child who questions initially may be one who requires considerable structuring of his assignments in order to work effectively. Questioning at the upper level may be merely normal doubting, or can shade into behavior suggesting a child who can not accept failure at any level. Questioning about "traumatic" material, such as certain Comprehension items, may suggest preoccupations which keep a child from functioning adequately in all areas.

There are various kinds of structuring remarks, such as, "Are there time limits?", "Do you want more than one answer?" or "Can I make up anything I want?" Remarks of this sort are an attempt to master the situation by establishing rules and thus gaining security. This behavior is characteristic of persons with obsessive and compulsive trends.

Situational Assessment

Responding to the many questions and items on the WISC requires the child to come up with a wide spectrum of information and experience. It is not surprising that a child may find himself momentarily at a loss in making these shifts. This can again be viewed on a continuum from a stopping to rally one's forces and assess the situation to the other extreme of blocking. Thus, the well-adjusted child may take a few seconds to come up with an answer or to look over the problem. However, when severe blocking occurs, so that "I don't know" is a frequent answer even at the simplest level, problems are suggested. The unwillingness to hazard an answer may indicate such alternatives as a perfectionistic self standard, apathy, little interest in the task, or a lack of emotional energy for use in intellectual tasks. In the latter case, repression has played too great a part in personality development. The effort spent to repress traumatic material has apparently spread to even innocuous aspects of the world. To clarify which personality variable is affected here, praise and encouragement are of importance. An answer which is readily given after encouragement has not apparently been adversely affected by the repressive process. It should be noted here that an inattentive or uninterested examiner may allow an anxious child to respond with an "I don't know" from the very beginning of the test. Failure to establish the meaning of this for the child—a momentary lapse, a fear of giving less than a perfect answer, for example—may lead to a test full of cryptic I-don't-know's and a calculated IQ which is far below the child's actual functioning level. Had the examiner encouraged the child to try, or guess, he could have discovered the point at which I-don't-know was the child's valid assessment of the upper limits of his knowledge rather than a meaningless catch phrase. Not to belabor the point, a test replete with I-don't-know's which is not followed by some attempt at eliciting an answer can never be valid or reliable.

Thoughtfulness

Less common than the above is a variable which ranges from an ideal of thoughtfulness to an extreme overdeliberateness. At the one extreme it indicates that the child is attending to the task at hand with care, in a positive manner, without becoming rattled or disorganized by difficulties. For example, he may stop to check a Block Design pattern to be sure no small error has remained. Yet at the other extreme, the child may ponder endlessly before hazarding a response. This behavior is penalized heavily on timed items and should be recorded. Failures due primarily to deliberateness may stem from fear of making a mistake or being "stupid." Used to extremes, deliberateness shades into obsessive and ambivalent doubting, and may be a forerunner of a serious personality problem. Perfectionism can be revealed in this way, and may prove to be an important lead to such school difficulties as inability to complete classroom assignments. Overdeliberateness should be distinguished from negativism: the former can be over come by urging the child to guess, while the latter merely becomes more firmly established with urging.

Hesitant remarks, such as, "Well, let's see," signify a reluctance to conform to the task (environmental demands) and yet a fear of crossing others. Excessive stalling remarks, such as, "I wonder," "it might," "perhaps," point in the direction of a cautious, self-doubting person. This is also shown by denial of the exactness of a response ("That's probably wrong!").

Persistence

The necessity to persist at a task until solved must be differentiated as one end of a continuum which ranges from normal persistence to useless stubbornness. At one point, persistence may be organized and realistic. For instance, several thoughtful alternatives might be explored on Block Design or Object Assembly. At the other extreme, effort may disintegrate into perseverative, unadaptive attempts to fit parts where they do not belong on Object Assembly, or rotate two blocks at the same time so that they never meet to make a pattern in Block Design.

Some children insist on attempting problems beyond their ability in a somewhat driven manner. The willingness to acknowledge one's limitations can be important and valuable in the classroom, which requires the acceptance of a state of ignorance in order to acquire learning. When a child is unable to admit that he does not know how to do something and needs help in acquiring the proper skills, he is unable to learn. Stubbornness can range from simple unproductive repetitive efforts to the extreme seen rarely in children and adults save those with severe brain damage, where the same response is given to each picture or question perseveratively. At the less extreme level, stubbornness can be a clue to the ability or inability of a child to organize activities within the time limits which are culturally imposed on most tasks. The significance of such behavior in the classroom is readily evident.

Acknowledgment of Limitations

Quite the reverse of the above is a continuum from the ability to acknowledge what one cannot do to the extreme of giving up without a struggle. The examiner who has a time limit is pleased to work with the child who tries hard, succeeds on a fair number of items and gradually reaches his upper limits, at which point he can say without concern, "I haven't learned that yet." The other extreme is the child who gives up, rejecting even easy problems as "too hard." Significant problems in learning may be indicated in the latter case. Giving up may mean the low level of aspiration so typical of the non-achiever, or it may indicate the child's real uncertainty and doubt of his own abilities. On occasion, specific neurological difficulties may lead to erratic skills, such as good verbal ability, but almost no success on items calling for use of a pencil, such as Coding. In such a situation, it may be difficult for a child to judge his own ability accurately. A child with such a problem often simply gives up rather than risk failures in areas he has never explored. Somewhat the same defensive behavior is seen in a child who tends toward a passive-aggressive role. This has been defined (Prelinger, 1964) as a tendency toward overt compliance and conformity accompanied by subtle, sneaky, accidental or behind-the-back aggression. A background of impatient parents and teachers who expect the right answer at once may have led the child to develop a "give-up" philosophy in order to escape unrealistic pressure. Needless to say, the acceptance of the "giving up" by examiner or teacher confirms to such a child the world's acknowledgment of his supposed inability. Another aspect of this is seen in a child's tendency to blame others for his difficulties: "You didn't give me enough pieces, it can't be done." Further, this may reflect a more basic passivity which makes learning difficult: here, the child is not impelled to take in or grasp knowledge.

REACTION TO SUCCESS: It is important to observe the child's reaction to his work. Some children cannot accept the examiner's approval or praise, or even the obvious evidence of their own success, becoming acutely uncomfortable, and driving themselves to further effort. This is in contrast to the other extreme, in which the child obviously enjoys his success and is thereby eager to try more problems. For some children, success is discounted as unimportant, the items are "too easy." The child's inability to accept his own skills suggests a driving conscience (or parent), taking the enjoyment out of learning by constantly raising the level of aspiration, giving the child no chance to rest on his laurels. An overzealous drive for achievement at all costs often arises from this setting, reflecting itself in chronic dissatisfaction with one's performance.

REACTION TO FAILURE: The child's reaction to failures can give important clues to his self-concept. At one extreme, these are accepted as inevitable if not desirable, and readily and philosophically put aside. At the other extreme, failures are so overwhelming that they transfer from one setting to another. Thus, one error may precipitate another: the child accepts failure as inevitable, and effort is discarded. Particularly on the WISC, with its spiral format, the child is soon given another chance on another subtest to show what he can do. At worst, he need fail only a few items on any one subtest before starting over with easy items on the next subtest. Therefore, a tendency for failure to carry over can be evaluated in terms of the effect of failures with one subtest on responses to the next. If there is much such carryover, an extremely fragile self-concept is suggested: any difficulty is used by the child to prove how inadequate he is. The effectiveness of praise and support for such an individual, and the point at which they are needed and are successful, allows important inferences as to the role of the teacher in encouraging the child's success. This area also gives a lead as to the child's frustration tolerance. Proper evaluation and acceptance of failures by the child should allow him to resume directed effort on the next subtest, thus not penalizing himself unduly through guilt.

Availability of Appropriate Experience

INTELLECTUALITY: To succeed on the WISC, the child must have available his intellectual skills. For good adjustment, it is necessary to set aside emotional concerns and solve his problems with logical interpretations. On the other hand, this approach can be carried to such an extreme that all feelings and emotions are rejected. When answers are pedantic and overly extended, with all possible aspects covered (for example, on Information: #9, Who discovered America?, "Some people say Christopher Columbus in 1492, but Leif Erickson came to America before that, and the Vikings came to Greenland, and . . ."), it may indicate the need to be in control of "dangerous situations" by use of the intellect, with a corresponding fear of feelings and emotions.

Since the WISC subtests call for some ability to bypass emotions, this response mode should be carefully evaluated to determine what is extreme or inappropriate intellectualization. Also, it should be noted at what point the child views the test situation as requiring such careful responses. The need to be right, to avoid any presumable "trick" aspects by covering everything, suggests that intellectual matters have a threatening quality. The attempt to give all possible answers in order to avoid being wrong can reach the extreme of obsessive preoccupation, with all sorts of alternatives introduced, indicating the extent of doubting and ambivalence characterizing the child's thinking. A suggested hypothesis stemming from this is that in the classroom the child feels threatened, and must therefore defend himself from fearful feelings and emotions.

USE OF PERSONAL EXPERIENCE: In order to succeed on the diverse items in the WISC, each child must draw upon his past experiences.

At the same time, it is essential to disengage himself from these events, so that only the significant aspect, that which relates to the problem at hand, is brought up. This leads to a continuum of behavior, from the child who can recall pertinent events and distill the essence of them to apply to the current problem, to the child who recalls personal concerns but is unable to disengage himself from these concerns in order to answer the question. Thus, when test material recurrently elicits some reference to the child's own life and activities, rather than problem-solving, persistent problems in these areas are implied. As an example: Comprehension: #1, What is the thing to do when you cut your finger?, "Hospital. I went to the hospital for my tonsils." Here, the child has lost track of the presenting problem. His over-reaction to the minor discomfort of a cut finger as something requiring hospitalization indicates poor judgment. It also suggests an inappropriate degree of self-centeredness typically seen in an immature personality or in a child who is unable to act in an age-adequate manner. Personal reference can be brought out in two ways: first, a pervasive flooding of personal material through-the test, and second, an unwarranted insertion of personal material into a specific area, suggesting that disturbances are limited to this aspect alone. Comprehension items may trigger such responses by their hostile or guilt-arousing content. An entire subtest which is handled with great difficulty may also illustrate the same problem. As has been noted, a degree of reliance on personal experience is necessary in order to succeed on the WISC. The pre-examination period of establishing rapport is important in ascertaining the child's present realistic concerns. For example, just before being examined, a child had seen a youngster badly cut in a fall on the playground. He showed his immediate preoccupation with this incident in the initial conversation, and again on the Comprehension cut-finger item. No other references of a personal nature occurred, and the child was correctly classified as well adjusted (Lambert and Zimmerman, 1964).

OPENNESS TO EXPERIENCES: Another shading of the above situation can be ranged on a continuum from openness to experience to a tendency toward free association. To succeed on the WISC, the child must be able to reassemble data learned in one setting and apply them in another. As an example, the Information item #15, Why does oil float on water?, is sometimes answered correctly by relatively young children because of their freedom to use an analogy based on other data. However, at the other extreme, the child may be at the mercy of irrelevant intrusive associations which he scatters through the protocol, perhaps revealing current concerns, or merely his inability to reject nonpertinent stimuli around him (Information: #8, How many days in a week?, "Seven, I have a red dress like those flowers"). Only very young children should be expected to elaborate their responses with a flood of loosely associated ideas. The limited attention span and self-centered immaturity implied by this are important findings. Sometimes bizarre interjections point up clearly the presence of serious personality problems (Comprehension: #5, What should you do if you see a train approaching a broken track?, "I would get killed, the train would run over everybody. They would get cut up. Everybody would be killed. My brother is in the hospital.")

FANTASY: Freedom to draw upon one's imagination and to avoid the straightjacket of conformity can be seen as one end of a continuum which ranges at the other extreme to a loss of reality. The child who can use his imagination to come up with new solutions to problems can be versatile in handling new situations.

On the other hand, an unbridled and wild imagination may cause a child to ignore the task to which he is assigned and dwell instead upon his own ideas.

This may seem no more than the verbalization of a self-centered youngster who is not likely to attend to the demands of others. However, when responses verge on the odd or bizarre, it can mean serious disturbance.

SUMMARY

An attempt has been made to delineate certain examiner and child variables not ordinarily considered in the analysis of objective intelligence testing. These qualitative factors permit valuable inferences to be drawn and can greatly enhance understanding of the individual child.

REFERENCES

Cieuat, V. J.: Examiner differences with the Stanford Binet IQ. *Percept. & Motor Skills* 1965, 20, 317-318.

Fromm, Erike: Projective aspects of intellectual testing. In Rabin, A. I. and Haworth, Mary R., Eds., *Projective Techniques with Children.* New York: Grune & Stratton, 1960.

Fromm, Erika, Hartmen, Lenore D. and Marschak, Marian: Children's intelligence tests as a measure of dynamic personality functioning. *Amer. J. Orthopsychiat.* 1957, 277, 134-144.

Lambert, Nadine M. and Zimmerman, Irla Lee: A study of the areas of agreement and disagreement among clinicians' ratings of school adjustment. *Amer. Psychol.* 1964, 19, 712.

Piotrowski, Z. A.: *Perceptanalysis.* New York: Macmillian, 1957.

Prelinger, E. and Zimet, C. N.: *An ego-psychological approach to character assessment.* New York: Free Press of Glencoe, 1964.

Rapaport, D., et al.: *Diagnostic Psychological Testing,* Vols I & II. Chicago: Year Book Publishers, 1946.

Schafer, R.: *The Clinical Application of Psychological Tests.* New York: International Universities Press, 1948.

Schafer, R.: *Psychoanalytic Interpretation in Rorschach Testing.* New York: Grune & Stratton, 1954.

Shapiro, D.: Special problems of testing borderline psychotics. *J. project. Tech.* 1954, 18, 387-394.

V

ADAPTATIONS AND BRIEF FORMS

Tests such as the Stanford Binet consist of different sorts of items grouped at each age level, with similar items thus not given to every child. The WISC has the distinct advantage of measuring each child serially on eleven different scales, with each section separately standardized. Two approaches have evolved which stem from this characteristic point scale construction. The first is to administer that portion of the test able to meet the needs of a specific group of children, relying on the standardization established for the various verbal and performance subtests. The second is to select a number of subtests or even individual items to be administered as a "brief" or incomplete WISC which can be used to estimate the full IQ of the child. Since a standard test is estimated to take 75 minutes to administer (Chambers, 1959), a brief test has distinct advantages where testing time is at a minimum. For purposes of discussion, the first approach will be called Selective-Partial WISC's, in that the test is limited to subtests most readily administered to certain children, while the second approach will be called Brief WISC's, in that the test is limited to combinations of subtests which best predict the total score, without specifying that these combinations apply to any particular group of children.

SELECTIVE-PARTIAL WISC's

Selective-Partial WISC's have been found useful for testing the handicapped (Braen and Mesling, 1959). The verbal scale can be used with blind subjects (Hayes, 1952; Scholl, 1953) or with orthopedically handicapped children (Hopkins et al., 1954). The performance scale can be used with deaf children, those with a speech defect, or the non-English speaking (Brill, 1962; Larr, 1959; Braen and Mesling, 1959).

A particular advantage of the WISC is that the most appropriate section of the test may be utilized as a measure or estimate of the child's most normally functioning abilities, while the other section may be utilized to estimate the degree of the child's handicap. For example, a child with cerebral palsy might do better on the verbal scale, while his functioning on the performance scale could give valuable information as to the degree of his handicap. Also, the extent to which a deaf or hard-of-hearing child has mastered verbal concepts can be roughly estimated by comparing his verbal and performance scale scores (Myklebust, 1960).

With severely handicapped children or those with multiple handicaps, such as the non-verbal, partially paralyzed child, standard tests are often useless. Since the WISC subtests allow for separate scores, it is occasionally possible to administer at least one subtest of the WISC, perhaps with some variation, such as a moving material in the way the child indicates on Block Design, Picture Arrangement, or Object Assembly, or accepting some form of pointing or multiple choice response on Picture Completion (Taylor, 1959). As inadequate as such testing may be, it often allows at least some hint of ability which can be measured and which might otherwise be overlooked.

With totally deaf children, non-verbal administration of the WISC performance scale may be needed. To study the effects of pantomime instruction, Graham and Shapiro (1953) administered this scale to three groups of children, using pantomime instructions with a group of deaf children and normal children, and standard instructions with a third group also consisting of normal children. Results suggested that the pantomime instructions were only slightly penalizing to both the normal and the deaf groups.

COMBINATION APPROACH

A variation in using the Selective-Partial WISC has been suggested by Taylor (1959). She has combined similar items from the WISC and other tests. In this approach, failures on specific subtests of the WISC can be explored by administering similar but easier items from the other tests. This is especially helpful on subtests which tend to have too few "easy" items. A number of WISC subtests are so limited in range that a zero performance will still give the younger child what is in effect a meaningless and gratuitous weighted score, which tell nothing of his abilities. Thus, a child who fails the Similarities subtest on the WISC may be administered the easier Similarities items from the Binet. Complete inability to cope with Block Designs can be explored by use of the Kohs Blocks or, more simply, by asking the child to copy the examiner's "bridge" (Binet) or six-block pyramid (Merrill Palmer). In any of the subtest areas mentioned, the new Wechsler Preschool and Primary Scale of Intelligence (1966) should be of considerable help in this type of extension testing.

TESTING THE LIMITS

Another approach to the WISC is to adapt items in order to understand the child's difficulty with certain sections. Volle (1957) has suggested "testing the limits" with the verbal WISC by altering the wording of items to see if the child can solve somewhat simplified items. Holland (1960) tested bilingual children by repeating instructions in Spanish when the child failed to respond to the original instruction. The "limits" approach proves helpful in understanding not only the child who tends to score at the lower level of the test, but may also give a better estimate of the potential of a very bright child who is penalized by the somewhat bureaucratized vocabulary of some advanced Comprehension items (note particularly "organized charity" and "government examinations"). Since the standard administration procedure has not been followed, the resulting improvement in score, if it occurs, may not be used as a valid measure of "IQ." However, the potential so indicated may point out the need for retesting the child with a more adequate instrument.

BRIEF FORMS

Probably the most common adaptations of the WISC are the brief forms. The WISC has particular advantages when used in this manner, especially when a rapid screening device is needed, or when intellectual factors per se are not assumed to be in question. In the latter case, the WISC might be administered as part of a larger test battery, such as is used in a Child Guidance Clinic. By the administration of the other subtests, the standard test can be completed either on the spot, or later, if, following further evaluation such as staffing of a child seen at a Child Guidance Clinic, the partial results warrant gathering further information. Those who score extremely low or show considerable deviation from one subtest to another can be tested in full.

The brief form of the Binet was determined by Terman and Merrill (1937) by omitting two of the six items at each age level, with a time saving of approximately 25 per cent. In contrast, the brief forms of the WISC have been established by independent studies using arbitrary selections of subtests. The time involved depends on the number of subtests used, but can result in a time saving of 50 per cent or more.

In some settings it is common to omit one or more of the WISC subtests, according to the whim of the examiner. Since the omitted subtests vary from examiner to examiner or from test to test, this cavalier kind of "brief testing" has little to recommend it. Such an approach is particularly disconcerting when the tests are later compiled to be used for research. A knowledgeable selection of subtests to be administered or omitted when attempting brief testing, not the erratic lack of method noted above, is to be recommended.

A brief WISC has been defined by Schwartz and Levitt (1960) as one in which six or fewer subtests are used to calculate the full IQ. This follows the rule that time saved when fewer than five of the eleven subtests are omitted does not seem sufficient to justify the violation of the WISC standard administration.

Current studies of Brief WISC's emphasize the correlation of the various combinations of subtests with the total number of subtests. The best brief WISC's are considered to be those which correlate best with the full IQ. This approach seems to be a carry-over from the Binet, where the omission of items in the brief form is based purely on their lesser discriminative value in predicting the total score. It ignores the potential value of serial subtesting. By selecting subtests purely on their statistical "weight" in determining the full scale IQ, other subtests which might provide valuable information about the child's approach to certain intellectual tasks may be omitted. When the net result is merely a very small increase in accuracy of measurement, this approach must be questioned.

Actually, brief forms are of most value when chosen to suit a particular purpose. While emphasis is placed on the overall IQ estimate, the Brief WISC offers additional specific advantages. For example, it can give a rapid measure of school skills (Information, Arithmetic), verbal problem-solving, (Comprehension, Similarities), or visual motor problems (Picture Completion, Block Design, Coding). Selecting a brief form which gives some estimate of both verbal and performance skills, of course, gives a more rounded picture of the child.

Brief Form Combinations

Current studies of brief forms can be considered under two headings. One consists of thorough checking of one or more previously selected combinations, using specific populations, such as mentally retarded school children. The other involves the calculation of all possible combinations of subtests, usually consisting of from 2 to 6 combinations.

The published brief forms of the Wechsler-Bellevue served as the model for initial WISC brief forms (Herring, 1952). However, a crucial change from this random approach followed McNemar's (1950) insistence on the determination of brief forms by utilizing Wechsler's original standardization samples. Pointing out that "valid validities" could never be achieved by using test results from *deviant* populations, McNemar published formulas allowing for rapid calculation of best combinations. These formulas allowed Wechsler's standardization samples to be used as reference groups for computing correlations between brief forms and the full scale. (The intercorrelations among the subtests given in the manual were employed for this purpose.) Using this formula with the Wechsler-Bellevue, McNemar demonstrated that the resulting coefficients were high for the standardization group. Actually, they proved to be higher than originally reported (Howard, 1958.)

In 1959, Bridges used this approach to calculate nomographs for computing the "validity" of WISC brief forms.

Also in 1959, Geuting used the same formulas to compute results for all possible combinations of three and four subtests of the WISC, calculated for ages 7½, 10½, and 13½, the ages for which correlation data is available. Later, Howard (undated) expanded this approach by combining every possible pair, trio, quartet, and quintet of subtests. Then, assuming that short or brief forms are most likely to be used for children not representative of the general population, he studied the best brief forms as applied to two small atypical samples. Accuracy seemed high in the cross-validation; the errors of prediction were found to be very similar to those of the standardization sample.

Three other studies used all combinations, but employed atypical samples. Enburg et al. (1961) reported all combinations of three, four and five subtests using a large sample of suspected emotionally disturbed children seen at a child guidance clinic. Schwartz and Levitt (1960) reported all possible combinations of two to six subtests using a sample of mentally retarded school children, two-thirds of whom were Negro. Osborne and Allen (1962) reported all possible triads for a large sample of retarded school children.

Other studies of brief forms of the WISC consist of a few, often arbitrarily selected, combinations which have been applied to various groups, including normal school children (Gainer, 1962; Guyol et al., undated), physically disabled (Wight and Sandry, 1962), emotionally disturbed (Nickols and Nickols, 1963; Simpson and Bridges, 1959; Yalowitz and Armstrong, 1955), gifted (Chamber, 1959; Thompson and Finley 1958), and, most often, mentally retarded children in schools or in institutions (Carlton and Stacey 1954; Finley and Thompson 1958; etc.). These studies are summarized in Tables 2 and 3. By referring to them the psychologist is able to consider the adequacy of a specific combination of subtests for various subpopulations.

A potentially important criticism of brief testing was advanced by Ross (1959). The method of test selection involves a comparison of the prorated score based on the combination of subtests chosen with the total test score. However, the method of gathering this material is by utilizing the full test administered in standard order. In other words, each child has been given a standard test, not a brief test. Noting this, Sosulski (1961) administered the WISC to two groups of mentally retarded school children. The first group was administered a brief form (Information, Picture Arrangement, Picture Completion, Block Design, Coding) first, and the WISC then completed. The second group was given a standard WISC. For the two groups, correlations of the brief form with the total test were identical.

Criticizing the earlier, somewhat haphazard approach to brief testing, Ross (1959) further suggested that the most valid brief test would be that most thoroughly evaluated: the complete verbal scale of the WISC. Certainly in a school setting there is much to recommend this approach. The correlation with the full scale is acceptable (.89 or better); the relationship to school success closely parallels findings with the Binet; and the total administration time is relatively short and predictable.

Selecting a Good Brief Test Combination

There are at present so many combinations reported in the literature that no one specific brief-form can be considered in preference to any other. However, one rule of thumb might be kept in mind. Schwartz and Levitt (1960) note that a correlation of .90 between the brief form and the full scale would result in an estimated error of 8.6 scale score units. In other words, the IQ calculated from the brief test would be no more than 9 IQ points above or below the "true" (full scale) IQ in two-thirds of the cases. (This is similar to the reliability coefficient of .91 between the test and retest with the Binet.) Therefore a correlation in the lower .90's should be a reasonable baseline of allowable error in prediction.

Reviewing the studies of brief tests, several generalizations can be made. First, the most reliable estimates of intelligence from brief tests occur in the middle age range (10½ years). This is to be expected, since the WISC is generally most stable at this point. Second, the use of fewer than four subtests in a brief form results in a fairly low coefficient of reliability (.70 to .90), and the size of the resulting error of measurement must be considered carefully before such brief combinations are employed. Also, Mumpower (1964) points out that the misclassification of children in terms of levels of intellectual functioning may run as high as one in four, even when the correlation of the brief and full forms is .95.

Perhaps the most meaningful criticism of the brief WISC with its eliminative procedures is that it results in the loss of important information regarding the child's functioning in various areas. Each examiner must seriously consider the significance of this loss as against the time to be saved by brief testing.

Using Howard's table of brief forms based on the WISC standardization data as a baseline, the following review of various combinations is attempted:

PAIRS: When two subtests are paired, correlations with the full IQ rarely reach a significant level (.90 or better). The ten best pairs based on the standardization data (Howard, undated) correlate with the full scale score from .81 to .91, with the top combinations revealing standard errors of estimate between 9.0 and 9.9.

If a correlation of .90 is used as a cutoff, no pair is a satisfactory predictor of the full IQ at ages 7½ and 13½, while only four combinations—*Vocabulary, Block Design; Arithmetic, Vocabulary; Information, Vocabulary;* and *Information, Block Design*—are acceptable at age 10½ (the age level at which most correlations tend to be highest) with correlations of .90 and .91. Of these four, *Vocabulary, Block Design* and *Information, Block Design* are among the best ten at the other age levels, with correlations of .82 and .81 at age 7½, and .89 and .88 at age 13½, respectively.

Schwartz and Levitt (1960) in a survey of all brief combinations for retarded school children, two thirds of whom were Negro, reported their ten best pair combinations as correlating between .71 and .79 with the total score, a level not adequate for accurate prediction. Of the four best combinations for the standardization sample at age 10½, two were cross validated by the Schwartz and Levitt findings, although with much lower correlations (*Arithmetic, Vocabulary,* .72; *Vocabulary, Block Design* .74). The fact that their sample used Negro children, a group not included in the WISC standardization, weakens the generality of their findings.

In another study of retarded children (Carleton and Stacey, 1954), eight pairs of subtests first used with the Wechsler-Bellevue were evaluated. Correlations were low, from .64 to .80, and included only one of the pairs from the survey studies just reported: *Arithmetic, Vocabulary,* .73.

One of the combinations rating high in the survey studies, *Vocabulary, Block Design,* was cross-validated specifically for a sample of emotionally disturbed children (Simpson and Bridges, 1959), a group for which brief intellectual testing is often required. In another study, the same combination was checked for children hospitalized for physical disabilities (Wight and Sandry, 1962). Both studies reported fairly accurate correlations of .87 and .91 respectively. These were surpassed in a study of "exceptional children" (mean IQ 86), where the correlation reached .95 (Mumpower, 1964).

In summary, most brief forms consisting of only two subtests do not adequately predict the full IQ. The combination of *Vocabulary, Block Design* is the most intensively studied pair reported, and has proved useful, correlating as high as .95 for a variety of samples. When mentally retarded school children are being screened, however, pairs may not be adequate. The youngest sample (age 7½) in the standardization group showed a much smaller correlation (.82) than did the middle age group (age 10½), suggesting that pairs should be reserved for use with older children who are not suspected of being retarded. With such children, the *Vocabulary, Block Design* pair appears useful even when emotionally disturbed and physically handicapped children are to be evaluated.

TRIOS: With the addition of a third subtest, correlations rise sharply in the normal group. The best ten trios reported for the standardization data (Howard, undated) ranged from .88 to .95. Two of the ten trios for age 7½ and all ten for ages 10½ and 13½ meet the criterion of .90, with the best combination for all three age levels revealing standard errors of 7.1 to 7.8.

A combination which is within the top ten at all age levels and also has been evaluated for specific samples is *Arithmetic, Vocabulary, Block Design,* which shows a correlation of .88, .94, and .92 at the three age levels 7½, 10½, and 13½ (standard error 7.8 for age 10½). The same combination is listed for two groups of mentally retarded school children (Schwartz and Levitt, 1960; Osborne and Allen, 1962) reaching only .82 and .84. One must bear in mind that the standard error is uncomfortably large with this low a correlation. When used with an emotionally disturbed sample, *Arithmetic, Vocabulary, Block Design* reached a correlation of .91 (Enburg et al., 1961).

Carlton and Stacey (1954) evaluated six trios based on Wechsler Bellevue brief forms. Correlations were low, ranging from .73 to .84, and none overlapped with the surveys just mentioned.

In summary, brief forms composed of three subtests can be adequate predictors of the full scale IQ. The combination *Arithmetic, Vocabulary, Block Design* (.91 to .94, standard error 7.8) which adds *Arithmetic* to the best pair mentioned previously is able to estimate the intelligence of normal children in the middle and upper ranges and also emotionally disturbed children. However, when applied to a mentally retarded group, the relationship to estimated full IQ is less dependable.

QUARTET: When four subtests are combined, the ten best combinations reveal correlations of .92 or better for the standardization data (Howard, undated) at all age levels, with a standard error of 6.2 to 6.6.

No one combination was among the best 10 for all three levels, but six occur at two different age levels.

By contrast with the standardization sample (Howard, undated), again the mentally retarded sample (Schwartz and Levitt, 1960) did not produce an adequate correlation for any of the best fifteen quartets listed, with correlations ranging from .87 to .89. Five overlap with at least one age level of the standardization sample.

The emotionally disturbed example (Enburg, 1961) listed 10 combinations, all of which reached a correlation of .94. Two combinations overlappped with the standardization study.

Carlton and Stacey (1954) reported on a mentally retarded sample using five combinations drawn from the published studies of the Wechsler-Bellevue. Correlations ran from .82 to .88, but not one combination mentioned was among the best quartets in any other study.

Seeking combinations which were best for the standardization sample and cross-validated with the severely retarded, the most satisfactory appeared to be *Information, Similarities, Picture Arrange-*

ment, Object Assembly, correlating at .95 for age 10½, and at .94 at age 13½ (standardization sample), while it reached .88 for the retarded sample. This quartet was not among the ten best predictors for the early age, nor was it cross-listed among the best predictors for emotionally disturbed (Enburg, 1961). However, another combination (*Information, Vocabulary, Picture Arrangement, Block Design* was among the best predictors at 7½ and 10½ (.92 and .95) and also an excellent predictor for the emotionally disturbed (.94). It was not mentioned for the retarded sample. Not surprisingly, no combination could be found which was among the best ten predictors for all three (standardized) age levels, the retarded, and the emotionally disturbed.

Apart from the above surveys, three studies reported on individual combinations. The last mentioned combination (*Information, Vocabulary, Picture Arrangement, Block Design*) had been arbitrarily selected and tested with an emotionally disturbed sample (Yalowitz and Armstrong, 1955), correlating at .57 for this group. However, as noted, this combination was quite adequate for both the standardization sample and another emotionally disturbed sample. Guyol (undated) investigated a combination *Arithmetic, Vocabulary, Picture Arrangement, Block Design* (note the similarity to the best duo and trio reported) with a large group of normal and possibly emotionally disturbed children, reporting correlations of .93 to .96 for the several samples collected. This same combination was among the best ten only for the youngest group (7½ in the standardization sample, .92). The same combination almost reached the criterion of .90, achieving a correlation of .89 for the mentally retarded group Schwartz and Levitt, 1960). A sample of children with school problems, half of whom were also emotionally disturbed, was checked with an arbitrary combination consisting of *Information, Arithmetic, Digit Span, Picture Completion*. Correlations reached .90 and .95, respectively (Nichols and Nichols, 1963).

In summary, the best brief forms of the WISC based on combinations of four subtests are generally quite adequate predictors for the full IQ, correlating with the full scale at .92 or better for both the standardization sample and emotionally disturbed sample. The mentally retarded group continued to yield results below the .90 cutoff. It is clear from the above review that many combinations at this level (four subtests) are useful for brief testing, although for the mentally retarded group brief forms are not nearly as satisfactory as with the other groups reported.

Information, Vocabulary, Picture Arrangement, Block Design proved to be a useful form for normal and emotionally disturbed children (.92 or better). The combination *Arithmetic, Vocabulary, Picture Arrangement, Block Design* was adequately tested with wide samples and also proved useful (.92 plus).

QUINTETS: The largest number of subtests which has been widely evaluated for brief testing is five. Best combinations at this age level readily meet the .90 criterion.

For the normal groups (Howard, undated), none of the top ten combinations correlate with the full scale score below. 94, and standard errors are uniformly below 6. Two combinations were in the top ten at all three age levels: *Information, Comprehension, Arithmetic, Picture Arrangement, Object Assembly* (.95, .96, .96; standard error 5.6 at age 10½), and *Comprehension, Arithmetic, Vocabulary, Picture Arrangement, Object Assembly* (.94 .96, .96). The same combinations are among the highest combinations for a retarded sample (Schwartz and Levitt, 1960), with correlations of .92 and .90 respectively. This is the first level of combinations which met the .90 cutoff for a retarded group.

While there is no overlap from standardization data to combinations listed by Enburg et al. (1961) for emotionally disturbed children, Enburg's ten best correlations are at .95 or better, so it might be assumed that a reasonably high correlation would also be obtained for such children.

Three arbitrarily selected combinations have been carefully tested with large samples of children. A brief combination selected for rapid screening of mentally retarded children, *Information, Picture Completion, Picture Arrangement, Block Design, Coding*, correlated at .90 with the full scale for two separate samples of mentally retarded school children, and .86 for a third group of institutionalized children. Howard did not find this combination within his best ten at any age level, but reported it separately as correlating at .95 for age 10½ (standard error 6.9).

A second arbitrarily chosen form has been used to select or screen gifted school children: *Information, Similarities, Picture Assembly, Picture Completion, Block Design* correlates .75 with the full scale for a curtailed range from 125 IQ up (Thompson and Finley, 1963). With such a low correlation it is not surprising that this combination was not reported in any other study.

In a third study of normal school children, the combination *Information, Arithmetic, Vocabulary, Picture Arrangement, Block Design* was calculated for samples of bright (IQ's 120-154), normal IQ 90-110) and dull (IQ 46-79) with correlations of .77, .93, and .81, respectively. This combination does not appear in any other study (Gainer, 1962).

Only one study (Zimmerman and Lambert, 1961) has reported the use of a brief test selected to measure personality aspects with no attempt to correlate results with the full scale. In a study of normal school children given a battery which included a brief WISC, the tests were used to predict school adjustment.

The combination *Information, Comprehension, Similarities, Picture Completion, Block Design* proved to be significant in estimating adjustment. The verbal subtests gave an excellent sample of the child's verbalizations. *Comprehension* frequently elicited personal references which could be used to predict the extent to which problems invaded intellectual functioning, while *Information* gave a rapid estimate of school learning. *Similarities* allowed an estimate of the effectiveness of functioning. The two performance measures revealed acting out tendencies and indicated possible perceptual problems. Interestingly, none of the published surveys lists this combination, although combinations including four out of five of the subtests are frequently utilized, and it can be assumed that the correlation would be around .90 with the full scale.

In summary, when five subtests are used to predict the full scale IQ, many combinations meet or surpass the .90 criterion. For example, both *Information, Comprehension, Arithmetic, Picture Arrangement, Object Assembly* and *Comprehension, Arithmetic, Vocabulary, Picture Arrangement, Object Assembly* correlated highly at all three age levels for the normal sample, and were almost as adequate for a retarded sample.

SUBTESTS. ABBREVIATIONS USED IN TABLES 2-4.

INFORMATION	I	PICTURE COMPLETION	PC
COMPREHENSION	C	PICTURE ARRANGEMENT	PA
ARITHMETIC	A	BLOCK DESIGN	BD
SIMILARITIES	S	OBJECT ASSEMBLY	OA
VOCABULARY	V	CODING	Co
DIGIT SPAN	D		

TABLE 2. BRIEF FORMS OF THE WISC—SURVEY STUDIES OF ALL POSSIBLE COMBINATIONS

Subtest Combinations	Standardization Sample	Correlation with full scale IQ	Reference

2 to 5 subtests
Method: McNemar general and special formula
	normal children
	WISC standardization sample:
	  mean IQ 100; SD 15
	  ages 7½; 10½; 13½
	  N–600
		best combinations (See Table 4)
		age 7½: (2) .83, to (5) .95
		age 10½: (2) .91, to (5) .97
			Howard (undated)

	cross-validation samples:
	institutionalized mentally retarded children
	  mean IQ 53; SD 7
	  Age 12-19; range 6 to 15
	"wayward girls"
	  mean IQ 81; SD 18
	  mean age 14-15; range 11 to 16
		age 13½: (2) .92, to (5) .96	

3 and 4 subtests Method: McNemar general formula	normal children WISC standardization sample: see above	see above	Geuting (1959)

2 to 6 subtests
Method: calculation
	mentally retarded school children:
	  68% negro; 32% white
	  mean IQ 70; SD–
	  range 50 to 80
	  mean age 13-4; SD–
	  range 9 to 15
	  N–177
		best combinations (See Table 4)
		(2) .79
		(3) .84
		(4) .89
		(5) .92
		(6) .94
			Schwartz & Levitt (1960)

Subtest Combinations	Standardization Sample	Correlation with full scale IQ	Reference
3 to 5 subtests Method: calculation	suspected emotionally disturbed children Child Guidance Clinic mean IQ 97; SD 15 range 70 plus mean age 11-3; SD— range 5 to 15 N–147	best combinations (See Table 4) (3) .93 (4) .94 (5) .96	Enburg et al. (1961)
3 subtests Method: calculation	mentally retarded school children mean IQ 70; SD— range— mean age 10-1; SD 1-7 range 7 to 13 N–240 cross-validation sample: mentally retarded school children and institutionalized mentally retarded children mean IQ 66; SD— range— mean age 10-1; SD— range 7 to 13 N–50	best combination (3) .88 V–PA–BD (3) .90 V–PA–BD	Osborne & Allen (1962)

TABLE 3. BRIEF FORMS OF THE WISC—VALIDATION OF PRESELECTED COMBINATIONS

Subtest Combinations	Standardization Sample	Correlation with full scale IQ	Reference
2 to 5 subtests: 21 combinations Criterion: survey of published WB brief forms (Herring, 1952)	suspected mentally retarded children referred to an institution mean IQ 68; SD 9 range 46 to 91 mean age 12-3; SD 1-10 range 7 to 16 N–365	best combinations (2) .80 V–PA (3) .84 C–A–PA (4) .88 I–PC–PA–Co (5) .88 C–A–S–D–PA C–A–PC–BD–Co	Carlton & Stacey (1954)
2 to 5 subtests: 4 combinations Criterion: subtests correlating best with full scale	institutionalized mentally retarded children mean IQ 75; SD 13 range 48 to 99 mean age 13-6; SD 2-6 range 8 to 15 N–133	best combinations (2) .87 A–PA (3) .91 A–PA–Co (4) .92 A–S–PA–Co (5) .96 A–S–PC–PA–Co	Smith (1959)
4 and 5 subtests: 3 combinations Criterion: mean deviation of subtest scores from full scale score	suspected emotionally disturbed children (Child Guidance Clinic) ½ personality problems, ½ school and learning problems mean IQ 96; SD– range 51 to 143 mean age 11-5; SD– range 5 to 15 N–229	.55 I–S–V–PA–BD .57 I–V–PA–BD .61 I–A–V–PA–BD	Yalowitz & Armstrong (1955)

Subtest Combinations	Standardization Sample	Correlation with full scale IQ	Reference
2 subtests: V–BD Criterion: standardization correlations used with McNemar's formula	suspected emotionally disturbed children (Child Guidance Clinic) mean IQ 95; SD 16 range 54 to 143 mean age 10-4; SD 2-2 range 5 to 16 N–120	.87 V–BD	Simpson & Bridges (1959)
Same (cross-validation): V–BD	"exceptional children," University Special Education Department mean IQ 86; SD 20 range 48 to 133 mean age 11-3; SD— range 7 to 16 N–50	.95 V–BD	Mumpower (1964)
Same (cross-validation): V–BD	children hospitalized for physical disabilities mean IQ 101; SD 19 range 50 to 140 mean age 9–11; SD 2–8 range 6 to 15 N–83	.91 V–BD	Wight & Sandry (1962)
4 subtests: A–V–PA–BD Criterion: 2 verbal & 2 performance subtests; Wherry Doolittle test selection method applied to standardization data	normal children (public school practicum tests), suspected emotionally disturbed children (Child Guidance Clinic), referred school children mean IQ 97; SD— range 46 plus mean age— range— N–473	.93 to .96 A–V–PA–BD	Guyol et al. (undated)

Subtest Combinations	Standardization Sample	Correlation with full scale IQ	Reference
4 subtests: I–A–D–PC Criterion: satisfactory estimate of adult schizophrenic intelligence on the Wechsler-Bellevue	children referred for school problems with and without emotional disturbances mean IQ 97; SD 18 range 51 to 144 mean age 10-2; SD– range– N–74	.90 I–A–D–PC .95 .96	Nichols & Nichols (1963)
5 subtests: I–PC–PA–BD–Co Criterion: best predict full scale IQ & conserve administration time; Wherry Doolittle method	mentally retarded school children mean IQ 68; SD 7 range 50 to 80 mean age 10-11; SD 1-6 range 8 to 13 N–309	.90 I–PC–PA–BD–Co S.E.E. 3.12 IQ pts	Finley & Thompson (1958)
same (cross-validation):	mentally retarded school children mean IQ 68; SD 7 range 50 to 80 mean age– range 8 to 13 N–173	.86 I–PC–PA–BD–Co	Thompson & Finley (1962)
same (cross-validation):	institutionalized mentally retarded children mean IQ 58; SD 8 range 46 to 81 mean age 12-7; SD 2 range 7 to 16 N–145	.86 I–PC–PA–BD–Co	Kilman & Fisher (1960)

Subtest Combinations	Standardization Sample	Correlation with full scale IQ	Reference
same (cross-validation):	mentally retarded school children group I: special subtests given 1st, test completed group II: standard test mean IQ } not available mean age N–80	.90 I–PC–PA–BD–Co (.85) (.84)	Sosulski (1961)
5 subtests: I–S–PC–PA–BD Criterion: Wherry Doolittle. test selection method	gifted school children (IQ 125 plus) mean IQ 134; SD 6 range 125 plus mean age 10-2; SD 1-2 range 8 to 13 N–400 (& 150 cross validation)	.75 I–S–PC–PA–BD	Thompson & Finley (1963)
5 subtests: I–A–V–PA–BD Criterion: administer in 30 minutes or less; greatest amount of information for teachers; correlates highest with full IQ of normal group	normal school children: CTMM IQ's bright–120 to 154 normal–80 to 119 dull–46 to 79 7 age levels ages range 6–12 N–300	.77 I–A–V–PA–BD .93 .81	Gainer (1962)
1 subtest: Vocabulary, alternate words only	suspected emotionally disturbed children (Child Guidance Clinic) mean IQ– range– 10 age groups, 10 each mean age– range 5 to 14 N–200	split half reliability only, .94	Armstrong (1955)

TABLE 4. BEST WISC BRIEF FORMS

BEST DUOS Normals (Howard) Ages			Cross-validation (Howard)	
7½	10½	13½	Retarded	"Wayward Girls"
V–PA .83*	V–BD .91†	V–BD .89†	V–OA .84	.86
V–OA .83	A–V .91	I–BD .88	V–PA .72*	.87
I–PA .83	I–V .90	I–OA .88	V–BD .86	.88†
I–OA .83	*I–BD* .90	S–BD .88	A–V .86	.90
V–BD .82†	V–PA .89*	I–PA .87	*I–BD* .81	.89
C–OA .81	C–A .88	S–OA .86		
A–PC .81	S–V .88	I–S .86		
A–BD .81	C–BD .88	C–OA .86		
I–BD .81	S–BD .88	C–BD .86		
C–A .81	I–OA .88	I–PC .86		
A–OA .81				
Retarded (Schwartz and Levitt)				
A–PA .79‡	PA–OA .72			
V–PA .75	I–OA .72			
S–PA .74	A–V .72			
V–BD .74†	V–OA .72			
I–PA .73	S–BD .71			

Italicized test combinations are listed at all three age levels.

* Suspected mentally retarded children (Carlton and Stacey, 1954) .80.
† Emotionally disturbed children (Simpson & Bridges, 1959) .87; physically handicapped children (Wight & Sandry, 1962) .91; "exceptional children" .95 (Mumpower, 1964).
‡ Institutionalized retarded children (Smith) .87.

BEST TRIOS

NORMALS (Howard)

	Ages	
7½	**10½**	**13½**
I–C–OA .90	I–V–BD .94	I–S–OA .93
C–A–OA .90	A–V–BD .94	I–C–OA .93
A–V–OA .89	S–V–BD .94	S–V–BD .92
I–V–OA .89	I–V–OA .94	I–S–BD .92
V–PA–BD .89*	C–A–BD .93	S–V–CA .92
I–PA–BD .88	I–C–BD .93	C–S–OA .92
A–V–BD .88	A–V–PC .93	I–V–OA .92
C–A–BD .88	A–V–PA .93	A–V–BD .92
C–V–OA .88	C–V–BD .93	I–PA–BD .92
I–C–PA .88	I–V–PA .93	I–V–BD .92

Cross-validation (Howard) Retarded "Wayward Girls"

I–C–OA	.86	.89
C–A–OA	.92	.93
I–V–BD	.87	.92
A–V–BD	.92	.90
I–S–OA	.88	.93

Mentally Retarded: School Children (Osborne & Allen)

	base group	validating group
I–V–OA	.87	.89
I–PA–OA	.88	.89
C–PA–BD	.88	.88
C–PA–Co	.87	.87
V–PC–BD	.88	.87
V–PA–BD	.88	.90
V–BD–OA	.87	.90
PC–PA–BD	.87	.87

Retarded (Schwartz & Levitt)

A–V–PA	.84
I–A–PA	.84
A–PA–OA	.83
A–S–PA	.83
A–PA–OA	.83
I–PA–OA	.82
S–V–BD	.82
V–PA–BD	.82*
A–PC–PA	.82
V–PA–OA	.82
S–PA–OA	.82
A–V–BD	.82

Emotionally Disturbed (Enburg)

I–C–BD	.93
C–A–BD	.92
I–V–BD	.92
I–S–BD	.92
A–S–BD	.92
S–V–BD	.92
C–V–BD	.91
C–S–BD	.91
C–S–BD	.91
I–V–OA	.91
A–V–BD	.91

* Mentally retarded school children (Osborne & Allen, 1962) .88 and .90.

BEST QUARTETS

NORMALS (Howard)

Ages		
7½	10½	13½
I–C–A–OA .93	I–V–PA–OA .96	I–C–PA–OA .95
C–A–V–OA .93	C–A–V–BD .96	S–V–BD–Co .95
A–V–PA–BD .92*	I–A–V–BD .95	I–S–BD–Co .95
C–A–S–OA .92	I–V–PA–BD .95	I–S–PC–Co .95
I–C–PA–OA .92	S–V–PA–BD .95	I–C–S–OA .94
I–C–V–OA .92	I–S–PA–OA .95	I–S–OA–Co .94
I–V–PA–BD .92	S–V–PA–OA .95	S–V–PC–Co .94
C–A–PA–BD .92	I–V–BD–Co .95	I–S–PA–OA .94
I–V–PA–OA .92	I–A–V–OA .95	I–S–PA–BD .94
I–C–S–OA .92	S–V–BD–Co .95	A–S–V–OA .94

Cross-validation (Howard) Retarded "Wayward Girls"	(Schwartz & Levitt) Retarded	Emotionally Disturbed (Enburg)
I–C–A–OA .94 .96	I–A–PA–OA .89	C–A–S–BD .94
C–A–V–OA .93 .94	C–A–PA–OA .89	I–A–PC–OA .94
C–A–PA–OA .91 .95	A–V–PA–BD .89*	I–C–PA–BD .94
C–A–V–BD .88 .94	A–V–PA–OA .88	I–V–PC–BD .94
I–C–PA–OA .93 .94	A–S–PA–OA .88	I–S–PA–BD .94
S–V–BD–Co .92 .94	I–A–PA–BD .88	I–C–BD–Co .94
	A–S–PA–BD .88	I–C–PC–BD .94
	V–PC–PA–Co .88	I–C–A–BD .94
	C–A–PA–BD .88	I–V–PA–BD .94
	A–PC–PA–Co .88	I–C–S–BD .94
	I–S–PA–OA .88	
	S–V–PA–BD .88	

* Normal and emotionally disturbed children (Guyol et al.) .93-.96

BEST QUINTETS
NORMALS (Howard)

Ages

7½		10½		13½	
I–C–A–PA–OA	.95	I–S–V–PA–OA	.97	S–V–PC–BD–Co	.96
I–C–A–PA–BD	.94	I–A–V–PA–OA	.97	I–C–A–PA–OA	.96
I–C–A–PC–OA	.94	C–A–V–PC–BD	.97	I–S–PC–BD–Co	.96
I–C–A–BD–OA	.94	I–C–A–PA–OA	.96	I–A–S–PA–OA	.96
S–V–PA–BD–Co	.94	C–A–V–BD–Co	.96	I–C–S–PA–OA	.96
I–C–V–PA–OA	.94	C–A–V–PA–BD	.96	I–S–PA–BD–Co	.96
C–A–S–V–OA	.94	A–S–V–PA–OA	.96	I–C–S–BD–OA	.96
C–A–V–PA–OA	.94	I–S–V–BD–Co	.96	C–A–V–BD–OA	.96
C–A–S–PA–BD	.94	C–A–V–PA–OA	.96	C–A–V–PA–OA	.96
I–C–A–V–OA	.94	I–S–V–PA–BD	.96	A–S–V–BD–OA	.96
		I–C–A–PC–BD	.96		
		I–PC–PA–BD–Co	.95*		

Cross-Validation (Howard)
Retarded "Wayward Girls"

7½			Retarded (Schwartz & Levitt) 10½		Emotionally Disturbed (Enburg) 13½	
I–C–A–PA–OA	.94	.97	A–V–PC–PA–Co	.92	C–A–S–BD–Co	.96
I–C–A–PA–BD	.87	.96	S–V–PC–PA–Co	.92	C–A–S–PA–BD	.96
I–S–V–PA–OA	.93	.95	I–C–A–PA–OA	.92	I–C–V–PC–OA	.96
I–A–V–PA–OA	.94	.97	I–A–S–PA–OA	.92	I–C–A–PC–BD	.96
S–V–PC–BD–Co	.95	.97	A–S–V–PA–BD	.92	I–C–V–PC–BD	.95
I–PC–PA–BD–Co	.91	.96*	A–S–PC–PA–Co.	.91†	I–C–S–BD–Co	.95
			I–A–V–PA–OA	.91	I–C–A–PA–BD	.95
			S–V–PC–BD–Co	.91	C–A–V–PC–BD	.95
			A–S–V–PPA–OA	.91	I–C–V–BD–OA	.95
			C–A–S–PA–OA	.91	I–C–S–PA–BD	.95
			C–A–PC–PA–Co	.91		
			C–A–V–PA–OA	.90		
			C–A–S–PA–BD	.90		

* Mentally retarded children (Finley & Thompson, 1958) .90 (added as cross-validation).
† Institutionalized mentally retarded children (Smith, 1959) .96.

SUMMARY

Brief testing is an important contribution to the WISC. The two primary uses of abbreviated WISC's have been discussed; the Selective-Partial WISC which is tailored to specific population groups and the Brief WISC which is a short form employed to obtain a quick and accurate prediction of what the total test score would be were there time to administer a full battery.

The selection of specific subtests, calling upon performance or verbal skills, allows the examiner to evaluate the child's intellectual functioning in desired areas. Erratic functioning on the subtests may limit the accuracy of prediction of the full IQ, but also can be considered a clear signal to complete the entire test. Combinations of four or more subtests are necessary to produce a reliable estimate of intelligence. When combinations of at least four subtests are employed, the resulting IQ's are reliable estimates of the full scale IQ, falling within plus or minus 9 points in two-thirds of the cases.

Worth noting is the remarkable lack of overlap among subtest combinations studied with different samples. Perhaps the suggestion of Ross (1959) is the one that makes most sense in discussing the Brief WISC. The complete verbal scale of the WISC is by far the most completely evaluated brief scale and as such is the most valid of all possible combinations.

To date, little has been done to discover brief tests which are rewarding in prediction of adjustment, rather than IQ alone. This area can be a valuable source of research.

REFERENCES

Armstrong, Renate: A reliability study of a short form of the WISC Vocabulary subtest. *J. clin. Psychol.* 1954, 10, 248-261.

Baumeister, A. A.: Use of the WISC with mental retardates: a review. *Amer. J. ment. Defic.* 1964, 69, 183-194.

Braen, B. B. and Masling, J. M.: Intelligence tests used with special groups of children. *Except. Child.* 1959, 26, 42-45.

Bridges, C. C.: Nomographs for computing the "validity" of WISC or WB short forms. *J. consult. Psychol.* 1959, 23, 453-454.

Brill, R. G.: The relationship of Wechsler IQs to academic achievement among deaf students. *Except. Child.* 1962, 28, 315-322.

Carleton, F. and Stacey, C. L.: Evaluation of selected short forms of the WISC. *J. clin. Psychol.* 1954, 10, 248-261.

Chambers, J. A.: Preliminary screening methods in the identification of intellectually superior children. *Except Child.* 1959, 26, 145-150.

Corman, M.: (Etude clinque des forms reduites de l'echelle d'intelligence de Wechsler pour infants) Clinical study of short forms of the WISC. *Rev. Psychol. appl.* 1962, 12, 33-48.

Enburg, R., Vowley, V. N. and Stone, Beth: Short forms of the WISC for use with emotionally disturbed children. *J. clin. Psychol.* 1961, 17, 280-284.

Finley, Carmen J. and Thompson, J.: An abbreviated WISC for use with educable mentally retarded. *Amer. J. ment. Defic.* 1958, 63, 473-480.

Gainer, W. L.: An abbreviated form of the WISC. Unpublished D. Ed. thesis, University of Pacific, 1962.

Geuting, Mary P.: Validities of abbreviated scales of the WISC. Unpublished Master's thesis, Fordham University, 1959.

Graham, E. F. and Shapiro, E.: Use of the performance scale of the WISC with the deaf child. *J. consult. Psychol.* 1953, 17, 396-398.

Guyol, D. M., Byrd, J. W. and Russell, H. E.: *A short form of the WISC.* Mimeo., possibly Med. Technicians' supplement to Armed Forces Med. Journal (undated).

Hayes, S. P.: First Regional Conference on Mental Measurement of the Blind. Perkins Institute of the Blind, Watertown, Mass., 1952.

Herring, F. H.: An evaluation of published short forms of the Wechsler Bellevue Scale. *J. consult. Psychol.* 1952, 16, 119-123.

Holland, W. R.: Language barrier as an educational problem of Spanish speaking children. *Except. Child.* 1960, 27, 42-47.

Hopkins, T. W., Bice, H. V. and Colton, Kathryn C.: *Evaluation and Educational of the Cerebral Palsied Child.* International Council Exceptional Children, Washington, D.C., 1954.

Howard, W.: A note on McNemar's "On abbreviated Wechsler-Bellevue Scales." *J. consult. Psychol.* 1958, 22, 414.

Howard, W.: WISC short form—full scale correlations in representative and atypical samples. Unpublished manuscript, undated.

Jastak, J. F. and Jastak, S. R.: Short forms of the WAIS and WISC. Vocabulary subtest. *J. clin. Psychol. Monog.*, 1964.

Kilman, Beverly A. and Fisher, G. M.: An evaluation of the Finley-Thompson abbreviations of the WISC for undifferentiated, brain damaged, and functional retardates. *Amer. J. ment. Defic.* 1960, 64, 742-746.

Larr, A. L. and Cain, E. R.: Measurement of native learning ability of deaf children. *Volta Rev.* 1959, 61, 160-162.

McNemar, Q.: On abbreviated Wechsler Bellevue Scales. *J. consult. Psychol.* 1950, 14, 79-81.

Mumpower, D. L.: The fallacy of the short form. *J. clin. Psychol.* 1964, 20, 111-113.

Myklebust, H.: *The Psychology of Deafness.* New York: Grune & Stratton, 1960.

Nickols, J. and Nickols, Marcia: Brief forms of the WISC for research. *J. clin. Psychol.* 1963, 19, 425.

Osborne, R. T. and Allen, J.: Validities of short forms of the WISC for mental retardates. *Psychol. Rep.* 1962, 11, 167-170.

Ross, A.: *The Practice of Clinical Child Psychology.* New York Grune & Stratton, 1959.

Scholl, Geraldine: Intellectual tests for visually handicapped children. *Except. Child.* 1953, 20, 116-120, 122-123.

Schwartz, L. and Levitt, E. E.: Short-forms of the WISC for children in the educable, non-institutionalized mentally retarded. *J. educ. Psychol.* 1960, 51, 187-190.

Simpson, W. H. and Bridges, C. C.: A short form of the WISC. *J. clin. Psychol.* 1959, 15, 424.

Smith, E. A.: A normative study of the WISC with high grade retarded boys. Unpublished paper. Wayne County Training School, Northville, Mich., 1959.

Sosulski, M. C.: A validation of the Finley-Thompson short form of the WISC for the educable mentally retarded. Unpublished Master's thesis. University of Windsor, Ontario, 1961.

Taylor, Edith M.: *Psychological Appraisal of Children with Cerebral Defects.* Cambridge, Mass.: Harvard University Press, 1959.

Terman, L. and Merrill, Maude *Measuring Intelligence.* New York: Houghton Mifflin, 1937.

Thompson, J. M. and Finley, Carmen J.: An abbreviated WISC for use with gifted elementary school children. *Calif. J. Educ. Res.* 1963, 23, 167-177.

Thompson, J. M. and Finley, Carmen J.: The validation of an abbreviated WISC for use with educable mentally retarded. *Educ. Psychol.* 1962, 22, 539-542.

Volle, F. O.: A proposal for testing the limits with mentally defective for purposes of subtest analysis of the WISC verbal scale. *J. clin. Psychol.* 1957, 13, 64-67.

Wechsler, D.: *Manual for the WISC.* New York: Psychological Corp., 1949.

Wight, B. W. and Sandry, M.: A short form of the WISC. *J. clin. Psychol.* 1962, 18, 166.

Yalowitz, J. M., and Armstrong, Renate B.: Validities of short forms of the WISC. *J. clin. Psychol.* 1955, 11, 275-277.

Yudin, L. W.: An abbreviated form of the WISC for use with emotionally disturbed children. *J. consult. Psychol.* 1966, 30, 272-275.

Zimmerman, Irla Lee and Lambert, Nadine: The relationship between individual psychological tests and school screening procedures for the identification of emotionally disturbed children. *Amer. Psychol.* 1961, 16, 370.

INDEX OF NAMES

Italics indicate references

INDEX OF SUBJECTS